FAITH, HOPE, AND *Love*

DEVOTIONAL

A 90-DAY
WALK WITH GOD

SHERRY & BOBBY **BURNETTE**

WHITAKER
HOUSE

Unless otherwise indicated, all Scripture quotations are taken from the *King James Version Easy Read Bible*, KJVER®, © 2001, 2007, 2010, 2015 by Whitaker House. Used by permission. All rights reserved. Scripture quotations marked (NKJV) are taken from the *New King James Version*, © 1979, 1980, 1982 by Thomas Nelson, Inc. Used by permission. All rights reserved.

The authors donate all royalties from this book to Love A Child, Inc., to help meet the needs of children in Haiti.

FAITH, HOPE, AND LOVE DEVOTIONAL
A 90-Day Walk with God

Sherry and Bobby Burnette
www.loveachild.com

ISBN: 978-1-64123-073-5
Printed in the United States of America
© 2018 by Sherry and Bobby Burnette

Whitaker House
1030 Hunt Valley Circle
New Kensington, PA 15068
www.whitakerhouse.com

4 5 6 7 8 9 10 11 12 **ᰃ** 25 24 23 22 21 20

Contents

Introduction

When we first came to Haiti in the 1970s, we never dreamed how far God would take us. If anyone had told us then what we would be doing now, we probably would have laughed like ninety-year-old Sarah did when she was told she would have a child!

But just as Sarah learned that nothing is too hard for God, so did we. The Bible teaches that we must first be faithful in smaller things before He trusts us with bigger things. God must have been pleased with us, as our ministry here has grown and includes more than we could ever have imagined.

And while it has always been a joy, it has not always been easy. One of the most important commitments we made was to rise early (usually 4:00 a.m.) and spend time together in prayer and God's Word. Each morning in His presence gives us the strength to face whatever the enemy throws at us that day and deepens the joy when we celebrate the day's victories.

Many of the thoughts in this book, *Faith, Hope, and Love Devotional: A 90-Day Walk with God*, came out of what God taught us during this precious time. Others came later in the day when God brought back to our hearts and minds the insights He had revealed to us in the morning hours. Our contact with God doesn't end with our devotional time. Rather, that time spent with Him becomes the foundation for our day. God tells us, *"Rejoice evermore. Pray without ceasing"* (1 Thessalonians 5:16–17). His grip on us is constant. Our connection to Him consists of us making His thoughts our thoughts and keeping them in the forefront of our minds all day long.

We started thinking about this book early in 2016. As we worked on the plans for it, God kept putting this verse on our hearts: *"And now abide faith, hope, love, these three; but the greatest of these is love"* (1 Corinthians 13:13 NKJV). And the reason for this became clear.

We could not have begun this journey in Haiti without faith in the God who put this dream and desire into our hearts. Our belief is in a great God who told us that with faith, all things are possible. That faith sustained us during times when it would have been easy to doubt that we were supposed to be here. Faith held us, kept us close, and pushed us along the path when our footsteps wavered.

Hope is frequently misunderstood and misinterpreted in our times. The kind of hope God gives is not a hope as in, "I 'hope' the weather will be nice tomorrow for the food distribution." God's hope is a sure thing, a knowing deep in our souls that compels us to keep working, to keep on being faithful, because we have the hope, the reality of eternal life given to us through our savior, Jesus. What we do and see in this life is only a cheap imitation of what God has waiting for us in glory! Hope helps us look past our circumstances because we keep our eyes fixed on the prize at the end of the race.

God saved the best and greatest for the end of the verse—His love. It is the glue that holds everything together. Without love, nothing else would matter, including faith and hope. Love created the universe and us, saved us from our sin, and propels us to love Him and all His creation in joyful thanksgiving! The love of God that fills our hearts and souls spills out of us and into the world and people around us. First Peter 4:8 tells us that *"love will cover a multitude of* sins" (NKJV). God's love covered our sins. Loving others covers their sin and gives us hearts of compassion for them—which is what led us to Haiti in the first place. After all, "Love Is Something You Do."

Faith, hope, and love—the three spiritual elements we need in our lives every day. While the lessons we've presented in this devotional were learned on the mission field, they are true for everyone, everywhere. This is the nature of God's truth. It works here in Haiti. It will work for you, wherever you are in the world.

The chorus of a familiar hymn contains this line, "And He walks with me, and He talks with me…." In Genesis 5:24, we read about Enoch, who walked so close to God that *"God took him."* In other words, Enoch never died—he just walked with God from this earth straight into heaven!

While this probably won't happen to any of us, our hearts do yearn to be closer to God. Our prayer is that these devotions will bless you, comfort you, and strengthen you as you take this ninety-day walk with God.

—*Bobby and Sherry Burnette*

For more information about our ministry, what's going on daily, and how you can help, email us at: info@LAChaiti.org, or go to our website: www.loveachild.com

Write to us at: Box 60063, Fort Myers, FL 33906.

To talk with one of our staff, call 239-210-6107.

DAY 1
Lord, What Do You Want Me to Do?

READ: JOSHUA 9:1–18

How many times have we not taken the time to ask the Lord for His advice and His guidance? When Bobby and I were first married, I would try to give him a little "wifely" advice. He would say, "Honey, I know what I'm doing." Through the years, we have both learned to pray and ask the Lord what He wants us to do.

Joshua had been anointed in the place of Moses. God promised to be with him, but the Lord wanted Joshua to pray first. In today's reading, Joshua and his men are tricked into making an alliance with their enemies, whom God wanted to destroy.

"And the men took of their victuals, and asked not counsel at the mouth of the LORD" (verse 14). Bad mistake. Today, as you have decisions facing you, ask the counsel of the Lord first. As many people have said, "Let Jesus take the wheel."

FOCUS FOR TODAY: Bring a decision with which you're struggling before the Lord, ask for His wisdom, then act.

DAY 2
God's Victory

READ: JOSHUA 10:1–15

Joshua had taken the place of Moses to lead the children of Israel. And now five kings of the Amorites were encamped close by, ready to make war against Gibeon. The Gibeonites called on Joshua for help. The Lord told Joshua, *"Fear them not: for I have delivered them into your hand"* (verse 8). Even though the Israelites were outnumbered, the Lord sent His angels, killed many of the enemy and chased the rest. But God didn't stop there. He rained huge hailstones from the sky and killed more. The Bible says, *"They were more which died with hailstones than they whom the children of Israel slew with the sword"* (verse 11).

Joshua and his army got involved. The battle was so intense and they were killing so many of the enemy, that Joshua commanded the sun to stand still, so the Israelites could finish them off. And it happened!

When it looks like the odds are stacked up against you, God has a miracle with your name on it. You are always on the winning side.

FOCUS FOR TODAY: Pray about a seemingly impossible situation in your life. Then, wait and watch for God's mighty hand to work its wonders.

DAY 3
Praise Him in the Dance

READ: PSALM 149

I grew up in a small country church. I never saw anyone dancing before the Lord. When I started dating Bobby, he told me about the time he got saved when he was sixteen years old. He would go into his bedroom, lock the door, and dance before the Lord, like David did when he brought the Ark of the Covenant back home. (See 2 Samuel 6:12–14.)

The woman who raised Bobby hated God and hated church. One day, she looked through the keyhole of his bedroom and saw Bobby dancing before the Lord. She took him before a judge in Orlando, Florida, to have him declared insane, like his mother, but he was just "crazy about Jesus"! After speaking with him, the judge decided Bobby was fine.

In our churches here in Haiti, even in our Love A Child Children's Home services, adults and children alike dance before the Lord with praise. I believe our heavenly Father loves to see us doing this! There is a time to "*be still, and know that* [He is] *God*" (Psalm 46:10) but there is also a time to "*praise His name in the dance*" (Psalm 149:3).

FOCUS FOR TODAY: If you are discouraged, or wrestling with a problem, put on your heavenly music. Praise Him in dance—because the battle is already won!

DAY 4
Nothing Is Too Hard for God

READ: PSALM 65

When I was two weeks old, my mother was committed to an insane asylum, where she stayed for twenty-one years. After all that time, the doctors and nurses probably had no hope for her to ever be any different. In her twenty-first year there, the Lord gave me a word that He would restore her mind and heal her before the year was over. And He did! For the next year, she lived with Sherry and me. Let me tell you, she had a better mind and more sense than I did.

It is so easy when we are on the mountaintop and everything is going well to say, "No, there's nothing, absolutely nothing, too hard for God." We can often forget that affirmation when we have loved ones being attacked by Satan mentally or physically, when we hear discouraging words from the doctor, when we experience alienation from a loved one, when we've lost our job—when any number of things go wrong.

Today, whatever you are dealing with, know that we serve a God who can make the impossible possible. Let's believe that together. *"I am the Lord, the God of all flesh: is there any thing too hard for Me?"* (Jeremiah 32:27).

FOCUS FOR TODAY: You can do everything that is possible and let God do the impossible.

DAY 5
Sacrificial Giving

READ: 2 SAMUEL 24:18–25

Because of David's sin, the Lord had sent a plague on the people of Israel. Gad, a prophet, told David that God wanted him to travel to Araunah the Jebusite to buy a threshing floor and offer a sacrifice there, so the Lord would remove the plague. Araunah runs to meet David to find out why he has come to his city. David replies, *"To buy the threshingfloor of you"* (verse 21).

Araunah tells David that he will not only give it to him, but will also include oxen, threshing instruments, wood, and anything else David might need. This was a great and generous thing for Araunah to do. But David said, *"Nay; but I will surely buy it of you at a price: neither will I offer burned offerings to the LORD my God of that which does cost me nothing"* (verse 24).

A sacrificial offering is something that will cost you, whether it is your time, your money, or your life. If you receive something for nothing and then turn around and give it to the Lord, it is neither sacrificial nor an offering.

FOCUS FOR TODAY: What can you give today that will cost you something? Live to give!

DAY 6
How Thirsty Are You?

READ: PSALM 42

As the hart pants after the water brooks, so pants my soul after You, O God" (verse 1). There is famine in many parts of Haiti now, due to the rain coming late. The ground has been dusty, and the mountains have been white and parched. Many times, Bobby and I have had to literally walk over a mountain because our vehicle broke down. I remember being so thirsty as the hot tropical sun beat down on me. Once, we ran out of water, and I thought, *Oh, Lord, if only I had a cup of water; I am so thirsty.*

Are you thirsty for the Lord? Do you desire to "drink of Him," more than anything in the world? Thirst after the Lord. He wants us to be so thirsty for Him, His love, and His Word that we pant for Him.

FOCUS FOR TODAY: Spend time in the Word and in the Lord's presence. He will quench your longing soul.

DAY 7
Out from Lo-Debar

READ: 2 SAMUEL 9:1–13

When Saul and his son, Jonathan, were killed in battle, David became king. Even though Saul had repeatedly sought to kill David, David had always promised Jonathan, his best friend, that he would show kindness to his family. After some time had passed, David learned that Jonathan had a son, Mephibosheth, who was still alive.

Mephibosheth was hiding from David in a small town called Lo-debar. Its name meant "without pasture." It was dry, barren and dusty, so there were no crops. Mephibosheth's circumstances were just as sad as this town's. Being a beggar and lame in both feet, with a grandfather who'd been David's number one enemy, left Mephibosheth feeling hopeless and fearing for his life.

David sent for Mephibosheth and extended great mercy. Not only did David restore his family's land to him, but he also included lots of servants to work the land for him, restoring Mephibosheth's fortune. Best of all, David brought Mephibosheth out of Lo-debar and declared that Mephibosheth would sit and eat at the king's table forever.

You may feel like you are in Lo-debar right now because of your finances, your children's problems, your marriage, or that job you hate. But there is good news: Jesus is getting ready to bring you out. You need to say, "Ha! Take that, devil! I'm coming out of Lo-debar. Jesus has made a way for me!"

FOCUS FOR TODAY: God never leaves you alone to waste away in a desolate place. He will deliver you in His time.

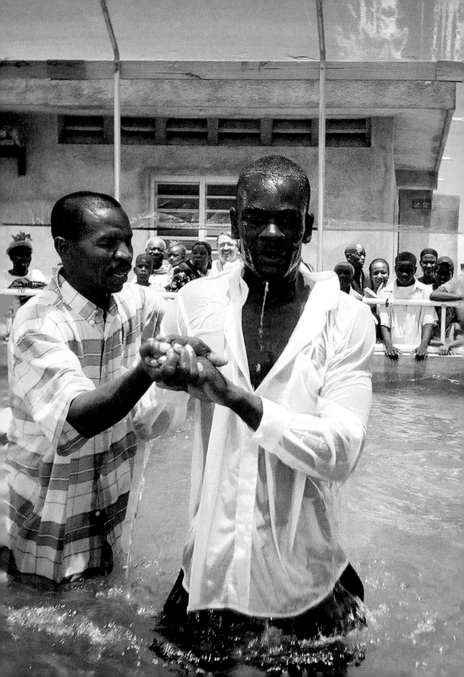

DAY 8
God Gave Him Another Heart

READ: 1 SAMUEL 10:1–9

Evangelist Oswald J. Smith once said, "We talk of the Second Coming; half the world has never heard of the first."

The people in many voodoo villages in Haiti do not know that Jesus died for them and that He can forgive their sins, heal their bodies, or remove their fears. When we conduct a mobile medical clinic in a voodoo village, or when we feed them, they can see the love of God, even before we speak. Our actions say more than our words.

I remember meeting an evil witch doctor named Joel years ago. We were using his tonnel—a round structure where voodoo services are held—for our mobile medical clinics. The Lord spoke to us and said, "Do not preach to him. Just live the life in front of him." And that's what we did. Before long, Joel came to me and said, "I want to belong to the same country you belong to." But he didn't mean the United States. He wanted to be a Christian. We prayed and he began to cry. When he got up off the ground, he said, "You will never see the old Joel again!" God gave him another heart.

FOCUS FOR TODAY: If you are trying to win someone to the Lord, let your actions speak louder than your words. God gave Saul another heart in today's reading and did likewise for our friend, Joel. He can give anyone another heart, "a clean heart," as the psalmist says.

DAY 9
The Lord Looks at Your Heart

READ: 1 SAMUEL 16:1–13

God sent Samuel to anoint one of Jesse's sons to be the next king. After looking at seven of them, the Lord said, *"For the LORD sees not as man sees; for man looks on the outward appearance, but the LORD looks on the heart"* (verse 7).

When we first moved to Haiti, we lived in Mt. Noire in the mountains. We had a young mechanic named Nelio. He was always fixing one of our junk trucks, which were constantly breaking down. One day, Nelio was working under the hood of our truck with his shirt off, sweat pouring down his back. He was covered with grease.

Bobby came over, stood beside me, and said, "See that young man, Nelio? God just spoke to me and said, 'He will run everything for Love A Child in Haiti.'"

I said, "Bobby, he can't speak English." But not long afterward, Nelio learned English quickly. Today, he is the Haitian Director of Love A Child. God could not have chosen anyone better. I'm so glad that God didn't judge him on the outside, but looked deep into his heart.

You may be the one that God has chosen simply because of your heart. Men only see the outside, but God sees the heart.

FOCUS FOR TODAY: Ask the Lord to help you focus more on what's inside people you know rather than what you see on the outside.

DAY 10
The Decoy

READ: JUDGES 16:4–21

In Judges 16, the devil sent a beautiful woman named Delilah to Samson. She wanted to discover the source of his strength. After she begged, pleaded, and heaven knows what else, Samson revealed his secret. Samson said, *"I will go out as at other times before, and shake myself. And he knew not that the LORD was departed from him"* (verse 20). Delilah had tricked him, making him unable to resist capture by the Philistines with whom she was aligned.

This not only cost him his relationship with the Lord, but he lost his sight when the Philistines gouged out his eyes. In the end, Samson repented, the Lord forgave him, and he killed more Philistines at his death than he had during his life.

Sometimes, the devil sends us a decoy. Maybe you were called of God to do something, but then you met that good-looking man or woman who pulled you off track. Or maybe it was a job or something else that at first seemed right in your own eyes.

Beware of the decoys the devil sends your way. Stay focused on the Lord and obey Him at all cost.

FOCUS FOR TODAY: Pray and seek God's guidance for every situation in your life so you can follow His path.

The Invisible Is More Real than the Visible

READ: 2 CORINTHIANS 4:13–18

One of the first things Bobby told me when we were dating as teenagers was that God had called him to go on a twenty-one-day fast. Once Bobby completed it, his ministry would begin. He tried for years to go the entire twenty-one days, but it was so hard. He could never seem to go more than a few days before quitting.

We were broke with two young children when finally, Bobby completed the twenty-one days of fasting—in a shack full of rats! That whole time, Bobby could not see or feel God, and God never spoke to him. The first night back home, as Bobby sat alone, God told him, *"The just shall walk by faith and not by sight"* (2 Corinthians 5:7).

Even when we cannot see or feel God's presence, He is still there. The heroes of our faith all lived simply, believing in an invisible God whom they could not see or touch. Look past the things you see with your natural eye. God has so much more in the supernatural, which the naked eye cannot see.

We believe more in the invisible than the visible!

FOCUS FOR TODAY: We all go through times when we can't feel God's presence, when He seems so far away. That's the time to rely on your faith!

DAY 12

Don't Use Someone Else's Armor

READ: 1 SAMUEL 17:32–50

David was probably about seventeen years old when he went out to fight the nine-foot-tall giant, Goliath. King Saul gave David his own armor to put on for the fight but David said, *"I cannot go with these; for I have not proved them"* (verse 39).

Saul's armor was heavy and David had never worn someone else's armor. However, he had experience using a sling and rocks. With them, he had killed a lion, a bear, and perhaps other wild animals as well. David was not afraid. He told Saul, *"The LORD that delivered me out of the paw of the lion, and out of the paw of the bear, He will deliver me out of the hand of this Philistine"* (verse 37).

People may suggest that you try to take on a giant their way, but what works for them may not work for you. God has already given you the things you need for the work He has called you to do. You have been through trials and know what works. You don't need to use someone else's armor.

FOCUS FOR TODAY: When you use what God has given you, that's all you need for victory.

DAY 13
All Will Be Restored

READ: 1 SAMUEL 30:1–20

When the Amalekites invaded David's city, Ziklag, David and his men had been in another city. They returned to find the city burned to the ground, their wives and children taken captive, and all their cattle, sheep, and everything else—gone. These grown men, who were warriors, first wept, then got angry at David and threatened to stone him. When David prayed, God allowed him and his army to defeat the enemy and *"David recovered all"* (verse 19).

Have you ever lost anything that was precious to you? Maybe you are one of those who were hit hard when hurricanes and flood waters took everything away. Or maybe you lost your job, or went through a divorce.

"And I will restore to you the years that the locust has eaten, the cankerworm, and the caterpillar, and the palmerworm" (Joel 2:25). In other words, God will restore the happiness you had.

He loves you so much. You may have lost everything or something precious, but God sees your future. It is blessed and it is bright. Don't be discouraged. God is the great restorer!

FOCUS FOR TODAY: Keep on serving Him and God will bless you with more than you had before.

DAY 14
Heart of Stone

READ: EZEKIEL 36:24–31

The people of Israel had rejected God again and again. They were at the point where their hearts had become as hard as the stone from which they fashioned the idols they worshipped. Yet God still reached out to them in love, giving them the solution to their hard hearts.

Then will I sprinkle clean water upon you, and you shall be clean…. A new heart also will I give you, and a new Spirit will I put within you: and I will take away the stony heart out of your flesh, and I will give you a heart of flesh. (verses 25–26)

Years ago, an elderly lady friend of ours shared a story. Her daughter had gotten pregnant, had a baby, and had to come home to stay with her parents. But the lady's husband was furious with his daughter because she'd had a child out of wedlock. Grandpa refused to hold the baby or talk to him. It broke Grandma's heart. So, she began to pray that God would give her husband another heart.

One day, as Grandpa walked by the cradle, he stopped and the baby smiled. He leaned down, picked up his grandson and hugged him. Then he cried. From that day on, the baby was Grandpa's boy.

There is no one bound by alcohol, drugs, hatred, or any other sin whom God cannot change. Know that God can give a new heart to that person you have been praying for.

FOCUS FOR TODAY: Pray for someone you love who needs their heart of stone changed to a heart of flesh.

DAY 15
Be Quiet

READ: 1 KINGS 19:9–12

We love to make a joyful noise and praise the Lord. There's nothing wrong with that, but there is a time and place for everything. Sometimes, we talk so much that we don't take time to be still and know that God is God. (See Psalm 46:10.)

Years ago, Bobby and I were at a Kathryn Kuhlman service. This great woman of God, now in glory, was an evangelist who had the gift of miracles. At her services, when she felt the Holy Spirit moving, she would make everyone be still so that the Spirit of God could move among the people.

Our six-month-old daughter, Julie, was sitting on my lap. At one point, she toppled over, bumped her head and started to cry. Immediately, the ushers came and asked me to take her out until she stopped, which I did. And of course, the Lord moved among the people.

Sometimes, we are so busy talking or thinking that we don't take a moment to sit in the quiet. Many times, the Lord speaks in a "still, small voice," such as Elijah heard. Take a moment each day to be still and listen.

FOCUS FOR TODAY: After reading today's scripture about Elijah, meditate on Psalm 46:10: *"Be still, and know that I am God."*

DAY 16
The Alabaster Box—Part One

READ: LUKE 7:36–48

Jesus gets an invitation to the house of a Pharisee named Simon. Under the law, the Jewish leaders were not allowed to eat with the common people, nor have anything to do with them, nor talk to a woman—especially not a certain kind of woman. We see in verse 37 that when Jesus sat down to eat, a prostitute went up behind Him, carrying an alabaster box of ointment. No doubt, she had either heard of Jesus or heard His words, which touched her heart.

> [She] *stood at His feet behind Him weeping, and began to wash His feet with tears, and did wipe them with the hairs of her head, and kissed His feet, and anointed them with the ointment.* (verse 38)

Perhaps it had been revealed to her that one day soon, this man would be nailed to a cross. His bare feet, dirty and dusty from walking in open sandals, were the closest thing she could touch. She wept so much that her tears were like water. She kissed His feet and poured expensive oil on them from her alabaster box. I imagine all of the people in the room heard her weeping and were embarrassed. Simon, being a Pharisee, immediately condemned her in his heart.

But what did Jesus say? (To be continued…)

FOCUS FOR TODAY: God never sees us as what we are. He sees us as what we can be. He looks deeper than we can imagine. He looks into our hearts and into our future.

DAY 17
The Alabaster Box—Part Two

READ: LUKE 7:39–50

As Simon thought about how bad this prostitute was, he assumed Jesus didn't know what kind of woman she was. But Jesus was about to turn the tables on Simon. Jesus first told him a story about forgiveness of debt. He then answered Simon's thoughts.

> *I entered into your house, you gave Me no water for My feet: but she has washed My feet with tears, and wiped them with the hairs of her head. You gave Me no kiss: but this woman since the time I came in has not ceased to kiss My feet. My head with oil you did not anoint: but this woman has anointed My feet with ointment.* (verses 44–46)

Then He told her, *"Your faith has saved you; go in peace"* (verse 50).

This one act of love and sincere repentance changed her forever. She came in with her life in broken pieces and left a new woman, because she did not care what people thought of her. She washed, kissed, and anointed the feet of the King of Kings.

Today, when the Lord leads you to do something for Him, perhaps an act of kindness, never be ashamed or afraid. Just do it! Take your "alabaster box" and do what God tells you to do.

FOCUS FOR TODAY: As you go about your day, keep your eyes and heart open for ways the Lord wants you to bless someone else. No action is too small when done with God's love in your heart!

DAY 18
What's Your Legacy?

READ: LUKE 16:19–31

In Luke 16, the story is told of a rich man and the poor beggar, Lazarus. The former was quite wealthy, dressed in purple and fine linen. The Bible says that he fared sumptuously (ate like a pig) every day. (See verse 19.)

Meanwhile, Lazarus, hungry, poor, and full of sores, laid at his gate, desiring only the crumbs that fell from the rich man's table. You know the story. The rich man died and went to hell, then Lazarus died and went to heaven. The rich man never thought about what he could or could not take with him when he died. He left nothing—not a giving heart, not compassion for the poor, nothing.

It's not what you take when you leave this world that's important—it's what you leave behind when you die that matters. In other words, what will be your legacy after you are gone? Some people who have everything leave nothing. Others have nothing but give, nonetheless. They leave everything.

FOCUS FOR TODAY: Think about what you want your legacy to be when you die. What do you want people to remember about you? As Christians, our goal is to hear Jesus say to us, *"Well done, you good and faithful servant…: enter you into the joy of your lord"* (Matthew 25:21).

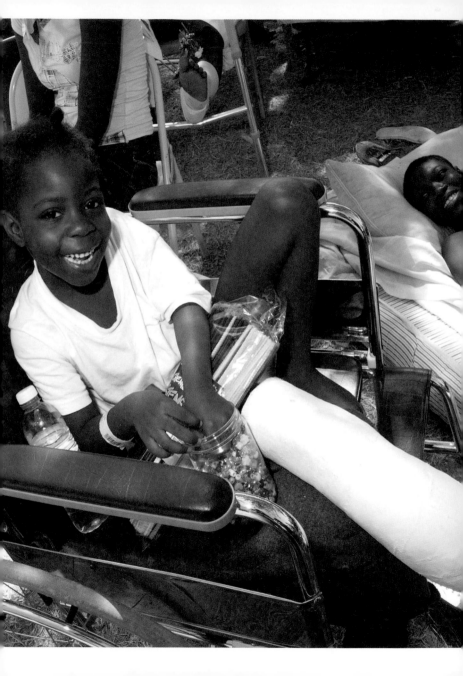

DAY 19
Losing What Matters

READ: ISAIAH 43:1–11

Have you ever felt as though you lost something you won't ever get back? Maybe you lost your job, your child to a wayward lifestyle, your house, or something else. With God, all things are possible. God is the great restorer.

When the poor people of Haiti were caught in the great earthquake of 2010, they lost everything. It looked like a bomb had been dropped. But many of them were praying people who had great faith in God, so they are now blessed. They survived and know they serve a God who can—and did—bring them through.

God is a restorer of everything, from broken hearts to material blessings. *"He said to the man, Stretch forth your hand. And he stretched it out: and his hand was restored whole as the other"* (Mark 3:5). Job lost everything, but all was returned to him and then some!

FOCUS FOR TODAY: Pray for people currently going through hard times. Stay in the Word and pray for strength and endurance for yourself when the going gets tough.

DAY 20
The Fourth Man in the Fire

READ: DANIEL 3:1–30

During the Babylonian exile, three young Hebrew men were thrown into a fiery furnace because they wouldn't bow down to a false god. It made Nebuchadnezzar so mad that he had the furnace heated seven times hotter than usual. The three friends were thrown into the furnace with all of their clothes on because the king wanted to make it utterly unbearable for them.

Nebuchadnezzar watched through a window and thought he would see them burnt to a crisp. What he saw instead surprised him. *"Lo, I see four men loose, walking in the midst of the fire, and they have no hurt; and the form of the fourth is like the Son of God"* (verse 25). When they came out of the furnace, the three young men didn't even have the smell of smoke on them!

You may be in a fiery furnace today that the devil has heated seven times hotter than normal. But if your spiritual eyes were opened, you would see Jesus walking with you. The Lord tells us we are not alone in this battle.

FOCUS FOR TODAY: Using a concordance—there are several free ones available online—look up the word *help* to read some of the promises God has given us. Choose one to memorize that speaks to your heart.

DAY 21
On the Move

READ: JOEL 2:28–32

When Bobby and I first met, there was such a move of God in the churches. It was nothing to hear a song sung with the anointing. People's hearts responded to the Holy Spirit and they were led to the altar. These days, many churches don't have altars to come to for prayer. Some don't even say anything about being born again. We have become too modern and sophisticated to let the Holy Spirit move, but I am thankful that God is still God! *"Having a form of godliness, but denying the power thereof: from such turn away"* (2 Timothy 3:5).

The Spirit of God is moving here in Haiti and in our children's home. Little children pray in the Spirit without anyone telling them to do so, lying on their faces, or with their hands outstretched to God. They pray for one another or come against an evil spirit. *"And on My servants and on My handmaidens I will pour out in those days of My Spirit"* (Acts 2:18).

If ever we needed God to move, it's now. Find a place to be filled that will satisfy your hunger and thirst for God. There are still faithful churches out there.

FOCUS FOR TODAY: Pray for God to lead you to a church that will feed your spirit, if you are not already in one. Pray that God would raise up church leaders who are true to God's Word. Ask the Lord to help you discern any false teachings.

DAY 22
Our God Is Great

READ: PSALM 97

What kind of God do we serve? Well, let's put it this way. God led one million people—men, women, and children—on a forty-year trip in the wilderness. There were no grocery stores in sight, no GPS to the Promised Land, and no clothing stores. In fact, their clothes actually had to grow as their bodies grew. The Bible says, *"And I have led you forty years in the wilderness: your clothes are not grown old upon you, and your shoe is not grown old upon your foot"* (Deuteronomy 29:5). God also provided manna, a supernatural food, to all of these people and caused water to gush from a rock.

Our tiny minds try to limit what God can do. We think He is not concerned about our daily bread or our daily problems. Why do we think He isn't big enough to meet our small needs? Think again and have a great day seeing your great God provide for you.

FOCUS FOR TODAY: Spend some time praising God in both word and song. Then pray for whatever needs you may have. Praise will build the faith you need to know that God is able to do anything for you.

Job's God—Part One

READ: JOB 1:13–22; JOB 2:7–13

God was so proud of Job and had so much confidence in him that He allowed Satan to test Job. In one single day, the Sabeans took all of Job's oxen and donkeys. Fire from heaven burned his sheep and his servants. Next, the Chaldeans came and took everything that was left.

At the same time, a great wind collapsed the house where all of his seven sons and three daughters were, killing all of them. Job got up, tore his clothes, shaved his head, fell to the ground and worshipped God. He put no blame on God but said, *"Blessed be the name of the LORD"* (Job 1:21).

His friends came to visit after hearing of his misfortune. Job was unrecognizable. In the distance, they saw a man, squatting on the ground, his head covered with dirt. Oozing boils covered his body, from the bottom of his feet to the top of his head. On the ground lay a piece of broken pottery with which he had been scraping and scratching himself. Once the wealthiest man in the east, Job was now reduced to ashes, poverty, and rotting flesh. When I read this, tears fill my eyes. Consider how he praised God in the midst of his tragedy, despite his wife encouraging him to curse God.

FOCUS FOR TODAY: It happens to us all, but when trials come, do we blame God or trust God? What was your view of and relationship with God during a difficult time? Stay tuned for "Part Two."

Job's God—Part Two

READ: JOB 42:10–17

In the 1950s, a great man of God named Jack Coe used to sing a song that included the verse, "Though God slay me, yet will I serve Him." He was talking about Job. After God allowed Satan to test Job, stealing everything he had, his friends should have prayed with him and encouraged him. The only other thing he had left was a nagging wife, who told him to *"curse God, and die"* (Job 2:9).

I cannot understand how Job could bear this trial. He had nothing to pass the time: no Bible, no television set, no iPad, no cell phone, no church to attend, no revivals. All he had was his faith in a God he had never seen. Job had a revelation that told him, *"When He has tried me, I shall come forth as gold"* (Job 23:10). And he did.

God healed Job and blessed him with twice as many sheep, camels, oxen, and donkeys as he had before. He became rich once again when all his friends showered him with gifts of gold. God also gave him seven sons and three daughters, ultimately living to see four generations of "Jobs"!

FOCUS FOR TODAY: If you are going through a crisis or difficult time, hang in there. God is going to bring you *"forth as gold"*!

DAY 25
Power over the Storms

READ: MATTHEW 14:22–33

Years ago, we had a team go to La Gonâve Island, a small island off the main coast of Haiti. After doing a mobile medical clinic, we had to take a small boat back to the mainland while facing an incoming storm. Then another storm rolled in and I was very concerned about our team. But we all began singing and praising the Lord! Suddenly, the Spirit of God filled the little boat—and we were immediately back on shore.

The disciples in today's reading faced a huge storm and were so terrified. Jesus could have come earlier, but as usual, He came right on time, walking on the water. When He did, the disciples became more afraid of the spirit walking toward them than they had been of the storm! He brought them peace saying, *"It is I; be not afraid"* (verse 27).

Today, you and I may be in the midst of a great life storm. Jesus comes to us just like He did for the disciples. Remember that Jesus is the eye of your storm. Believe Him when He says, *"Be not afraid"*!

FOCUS FOR TODAY: Sometimes, we are so afraid, all we can do is pray, "Help!" Pray today that Jesus will take away your fears and replace them with trust in His power.

DAY 26
The Calling to the Poor

READ: LUKE 14:12–14

Years ago, we were invited to a holiday party given by a wealthy lady in Haiti. We looked around and everyone there was very rich. There was not one person at the party who was poor.

What would happen if we threw a party and invited the poor, those who don't have nice clothes, or food to eat? It would probably be the best day of our lives.

And the stranger, and the fatherless, and the widow, which are inside your gates, shall come, and shall eat and be satisfied; that the LORD your God may bless you in all the work of your hand which you do. (Deuteronomy 14:29)

It has always been God's plan for His people to take care of the hungry, the orphans, and the stranger. There is no greater blessing in this world that can fill every crack in your heart and soul than feeding and caring for the poor. Let's be sensitive to the Spirit of God wherever we are. God may show you that one person He wants you to help today.

FOCUS FOR TODAY: Pray for the Lord to open your eyes so that you may recognize the needy you encounter today. Answer God's call to help.

DAY 27
Fiery Trials

READ: 1 PETER 1:3–9

When we moved to Haiti in July of 1991, we found ourselves in the midst of a great embargo. That meant nothing came in and nothing went out. No planes, no fuel, no imports—nothing. We had very little electricity for three years and had to learn to live by candlelight. People were killed. Our lives were threatened. Many missionaries left.

It was a test to see if we loved the Lord more than our families, friends, or anything else. It was not easy.

This was a fiery trial as referred to in today's reading:

That the trial of your faith, being much more precious than of gold that perishes, though it be tried with fire, might be found to praise and honor and glory at the appearing of Jesus Christ.

(verse 7)

Today, you may be in the fire because God wants to know if you love Him and trust Him more than anything else in the world. And you do! When He takes you through your trials and brings you out, you will be refined like pure gold, having greater faith. Know that after the crisis comes the blessing.

FOCUS FOR TODAY: Ask God for faith and perseverance during trials, especially if you are currently in one. Remember that God promises not to remove our trials, but to walk with us through them.

DAY 28
It's Not the Fall that Counts

READ: PSALM 37:21–34

Did you ever have a bad fall? We work with a village called Savaan Roche. It's full of rocks and shaped like a teacup. You have to climb up to the rim of a mountain and look way down below. There is Savaan Roche, at the bottom of the teacup. The trip down is treacherous because there are millions of small rocks on top of slippery, loose ground. Team members always fall many times. One pastor's wife just sat and scooted all the way down.

All of us fall sometime in our lives, but God is always there.

The steps of a good man are ordered by the LORD: and He delights in his way. Though he fall, he shall not be utterly cast down: for the LORD upholds him with His hand.

(verses 23–24)

Don't give up. Press on toward the mark, even when it is hard. Be steadfast because our work for the Lord is not in vain.

FOCUS FOR TODAY: Remember, it's not the fall that counts, but whether you get back up. Arise, for He is there with you.

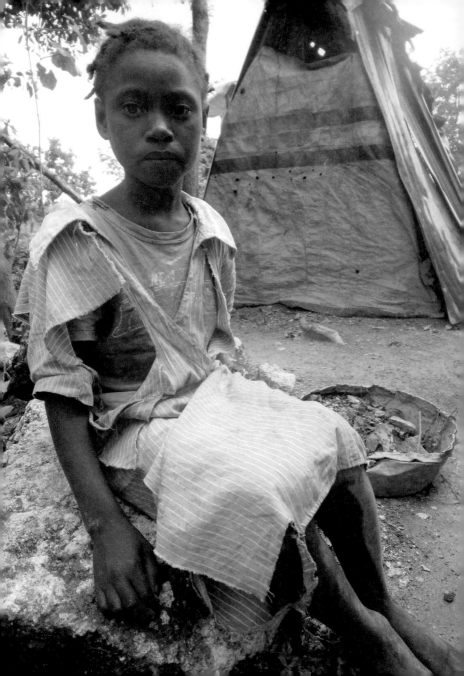

DAY 29
You're Not Home Yet

READ: EPHESIANS 2:19–22

I heard a story years ago about a great man of God. He was an elderly missionary, finally returning home after many years of ministry in a foreign country. He had fought the devil, survived many sicknesses, been away from family and friends for years, and won many to the Lord.

The plane had to make a stop on the way home. Some dignitary got off the plane. A crowd met him and a band played. When the missionary arrived home, there was not one person to meet him. Tears filled his eyes. Then the Lord spoke to him: "You're not home, yet."

None of us are home yet. We still serve on the front lines. *"I go to prepare a place for you. And if I go and prepare a place for you, I will come again, and receive you to Myself; that where I am, there you may be also"* (John 14:2–3). Someday we will arrive home and the reception will be glorious!

FOCUS FOR TODAY: As you journey through this life, pray to leave a trail paved with the love of Christ that leads to our heavenly and true home.

DAY 30
It's Time to Move On

READ: DEUTERONOMY 1:1–8

It had been forty years since the Israelites left Egypt. Over the years, they grumbled, complained and believed the ten spies who said that the Canaanites were too big and scary to conquer. They rebelled, and were punished. But life in the desert was all these people knew. In Horeb, the Lord said, *"You have dwelled long enough in this mount: turn you, and take your journey…. Behold, I have set the land before you"* (verses 6–8).

We often make the mistake of staying too long or getting too comfortable in one area of our life, when God wants us to move on. We get used to things and don't like to make changes. But change comes to all of us. Nothing stays the same.

Sometimes, fear holds us back. It becomes hard to make decisions, to move from one place to another, from one job to another, or to take bold, new steps. Maybe we are afraid of failing, but God is surely able to get us back on track if we do.

Knowing when it's time to move on is important. You will never know what is beyond your mountain, or the right place for you, until you make a move. Otherwise, you risk missing the blessings ahead.

FOCUS FOR TODAY: Take a look at your life. Determine places where God would like you to make changes. Start today, moving on with His help and guidance.

DAY 31
Still Thirsting for God

READ: PSALM 63

We have worked in Haiti for many years and I can clearly remember the day of the greatest thirst in my life. Our team had to go to one of our hardest-to-reach villages. Traveling in our four-wheel-drive vehicles for four hours, we got to the point where they could go no further. We then walked for miles up a mountain, something akin to torture in the heat of the day. But the trip back was worse. With the sun beating down on us, we ran out of water.

Now we were thirsty, dehydrated, and exhausted. All we could think about was getting some water. Finally, we reached a river and sat down to cool our feet. That's when we discovered Nelio, our Haitian director, had sent a man with a cooler full of ice, water, and soft drinks! We almost died and went to heaven right then.

The Lord wants us to be thirsty for Him in the same way. In many of the Psalms, David compared physical thirst to his soul's thirst for God. David said, *"O God, You are my God; early will I seek You: my soul thirsts for You, my flesh longs for You in a dry and thirsty land, where no water is"* (verse 1).

FOCUS FOR TODAY: We experience physical thirst every day that must be quenched with water. Quench your soul's thirst for God by seeking Him and reading His Word.

DAY 32
Open Doors

READ: ROMANS 8:31–37

When God gave the Promised Land to Moses and Joshua, they soon found out they would have many adversaries. They had to fight the giants, Canaanites, Hittites, Hivites, and Amorites. They had to face cities with high walls. This was just for starters! They won the victory because the Lord was with them.

When I was much younger in the Lord, I used to think that when the Lord made a promise, called me, or opened a wonderful door, I would just step into His will without any battles. I soon found out how wrong I was.

As missionaries, we've found the open door can be an opportunity to take food across mountains to a village of starving children, or build a church in an impossible situation. While we always pray for an open door, we must be aware there will be many adversaries.

They come in many shapes and forms. Vehicles break down, funds run out, or roads are too muddy to drive on. Your adversaries might be financial or physical problems, spirits of discouragement, or people, sometimes even within your own family. God's people always press their way in. Where God guides, He protects. The Lord is with you and me. Let's take what God says we can have.

FOCUS FOR TODAY: Pray that when you are doing what God wants you to do, you can be discerning of the enemy and the attacks against you. Ask for perseverance and victory.

DAY 33
Bad News

READ: ISAIAH 38:1–8

Imagine how you would feel if a prophet, a man of God, came to you and said, *"Set your house in order: for you shall die, and not live"* (verse 1). Isaiah, the prophet of God, went to King Hezekiah and spoke this death sentence over him.

Some years ago, I made Bobby go to a dermatologist in the states. He told Bobby, "You have melanoma and about six months to live." That was Bobby's death sentence. We did what King Hezekiah did. *"Then Hezekiah turned his face toward the wall, and prayed to the LORD"* (verse 2). God reversed the decision. He did the same thing for Bobby.

When we receive bad news, we must learn to turn our face to the wall and call on the same God that Abraham, Isaac, Jacob, Moses, Daniel, Paul, and many others in the Bible prayed to. We serve a God who still works miracles today. No matter how bad things look, all it takes is one touch from God. Our days can be faith-filled because we know the "God who can."

FOCUS FOR TODAY: Intercede for someone you know who is in need of a reversal in their current situation.

DAY 34
One Small Light

READ: JOHN 1:1–9

For our first three years in Haiti, we had very little electricity, living mostly by candlelight. I remember how dark the whole house was until one candle was lit. It was amazing what that single candle could do. It would light up the whole room. We could go up and down the stairs. Even when we went to the mountains, one candle gave off enough light for us to see the path.

But when it went it out, everything became dark and dangerous. Jesus said, *"Neither do men light a candle, and put it under a bushel"* (Matthew 5:15). The resulting darkness is the same. It may as well not have been lit at all.

Our light is the light of Jesus. Let your light shine today in the middle of this dark world. Shine in the grocery store, in the bank, in school, or wherever you are. You may be the only candle to many around you.

FOCUS FOR TODAY: Light your candle, because someone is always near you, watching you, and needing that light!

DAY 35
Cornelius: A Heart for the Poor

READ: ACTS 10:1–8, 25–34

There are three kinds of giving: tithes, offerings, and alms, which means giving to the poor. God blesses all of these, but I believe there is a special place in God's heart for those who go the second mile and give to those who cannot give back.

In Acts, we hear about a man named Cornelius. He was a Gentile, a Roman centurion, a believer in and follower of the Jewish God, and a giver of alms. It was in his giving of alms that God saw his heart. He sent Peter to preach to Cornelius so he could now become a follower of Jesus.

Cornelius was *"a devout man, and one that feared God with all his house, which gave much alms to the people, and prayed to God always"* (verse 2). And God said to him, *"Your prayers and your alms are come up for a memorial before God"* (verse 4).

Jesus told us we will always have the poor. In Deuteronomy 15:11, God commands us to help our poor and needy brothers. If we honor the Lord with what we have by blessing others, the Lord will bless us. Don't be afraid to give. Just like Cornelius gave his alms and was blessed with the greatest gift—salvation—God will bless you for your obedience.

FOCUS FOR TODAY: Even if you don't have much, when you see someone in need today, give what you can.

DAY 36
God's Invisible Army

READ: 2 KINGS 6:11–17

The armies of Syria had surrounded Israel. Elisha's servant looked out, saw all the chariots and horses, and was afraid. He said to Elisha, "What shall we do?" Then Elisha prayed for God to open the servant's eyes. When the Lord did this, the servant saw God's great army of fiery horses and chariots on the mountains above the Syrian army.

There have been countless times here in Haiti when we faced things like crazed men wearing red (*mouchwa*) scarves around their heads, blocking the road, and carrying burning tires and containers of gasoline. Other times, we've felt the physical presence of evil coming from witch doctors and voodoo men. This is when fear meets faith in God. *"They that be with us are more than they that be with them"* (verse 16).

We are not afraid of them. God is with us. Do not fear those people who are out to get you, trying to take your job, your faith, or whatever. The Lord will fight for you. When God is on your side, you are the winner.

FOCUS FOR TODAY: God's wonderful, invisible army is fighting for you and protecting you. God is greater than anything you face today or any day.

DAY 37
Decisions, Decisions

READ: 2 KINGS 7:3–8

The king of Syria had fought against the city of Samaria. To make matters worse, Samaria was experiencing a horrible famine. Four lepers who sat outside the city gate had to make a decision. Should they go into Samaria, where they would starve to death; stay outside the city, where they would also die; or go to the camp of the Syrians, where there was food but the risk of capture? They said, *"Why sit we here until we die?"* (verse 3).

They made the decision to fall into the hands of the Syrians. However, the Lord had just filled the Syrian camp with the sound of many chariots approaching. Thinking they were being attacked, all the Syrians fled. The lepers found food, drink, clothing, silver and gold. Then they went back to Samaria and told the others what they had found.

Years ago, Sherry and I started our ministry by preaching on the street corners in different towns. In the beginning, we struggled to make a decision as to which street corner to minister on. We were so afraid of making the wrong decision. I went to a man of God for guidance. The man said, "God can't bless you until you make a decision."

There may be famine and enemies in the city, but we have to make a decision. Don't be afraid. God will help you, but you must take the first step in faith.

FOCUS FOR TODAY: Pray about a decision you need to make in your life, then step out in faith.

DAY 38
Crybabies

READ: NUMBERS 13:26–14:1

When the people got the scary report from the ten spies with no faith, they cried all night long. Isn't it something? They forgot about the miracles of the ten plagues and how God kept them safe. They forgot about crossing the Red Sea on dry land, God's destruction of the Egyptian army, and how God fed a million people in the middle of a desert. They forgot about the water coming from the rock, and the cloud leading them by day, and the pillar of fire by night. All they could see were the giants.

Joshua and Caleb, the only two of the twelve spies who had great faith, could only see their powerful God. *"And Caleb stilled the people before Moses, and said, Let us go up at once, and possess it; for we are well able to overcome it"* (Numbers 13:30). But because Caleb and Joshua were the only men with faith, the people of Israel had to wander in the desert for forty years. Then God finally let them reach their destination, helped them to overcome the giants, and allowed them to possess the land.

Don't be a crybaby like the Israelites. No matter what you may be facing today, don't forget what God has already done for you. Praise Him, move forward, and be a giant killer.

FOCUS FOR TODAY: God has given you a promise. Go in and possess what God has said is yours.

DAY 39
A Virtuous Woman

READ: PROVERBS 31:10–31

This passage describes the virtuous woman. While I don't think I could ever measure up to this standard, my mother did. She lived with my father, an alcoholic, for over fifty years. She refused to give up on him. Each night, she did Bible devotions with all five of us kids. She made sure we went to church, even though Dad hated that Mom took us there. When there were no groceries in the house, she knelt down and prayed. Before long, someone would knock on the door and give us food.

Through everything, Mom could have hated Dad. Instead she loved him, all the way to his death. Right before Dad died, he finally accepted Jesus. *"Hatred stirs up strifes: but love covers all sins"* (Proverbs 10:12).

Mom is now in heaven, and I am sure Dad was the second one to meet my mother at the gates of heaven. Because of her, I am where I am today. All of us children turned out to be good parents and serve the Lord. *"Her children arise up, and call her blessed"* (Proverbs 31:28).

If your mother is still here on earth, be sure to tell her how much she means to you. God loves mothers!

FOCUS FOR TODAY: Thank God for your mother. If you don't have a good relationship with her, love her anyway and pray that God would change her heart and yours. Love her into the kingdom!

DAY 40
The Dreamer

READ: GENESIS 41:39–46

Joseph was seventeen years old when he had his first two dreams, and also was given the gift of dream interpretation. He recognized his dreams meant that in the future, his father and all of his brothers would bow down to him. This news did not go over well with his brothers.

For a long time, it seemed as though this would never happen. Joseph's brothers threw him into a pit and sold him to Egyptian slave traders. He became a slave to Potiphar and was imprisoned for years, even though he was innocent of any wrongdoing.

When Joseph was thirty years old, he stood before Pharaoh, who made Joseph governor over Egypt and put all power in his hands. Joseph's word became the law of the land. Why did Pharaoh do this? Because Joseph was the only person able to interpret his dreams. And now, the message in Joseph's dreams had finally come true.

Some people want to tear your dreams down, not build your dreams up. Let's be dream builders and encourage people to achieve their fullest potential for the Lord. Don't let anyone or anything stop your dream! What the Lord has put in your heart, He will bring to completion.

FOCUS FOR TODAY: Starting today, take as many days as you need to read about Joseph in Genesis 37 through Genesis 50. What an amazing and inspiring story!

DAY 41
Not Deciding Is a Decision

READ: PROVERBS 2:1–8

We make decisions each day of our lives. We used to have a friend who could never make a decision. She was always waiting for God to speak to her in a voice and tell her what to do. In reality, she used her spirituality as an excuse to not make a decision.

While it is important to pray about making the right decisions, God promised to grant us the wisdom we need to work for Him. You may be in the valley of making an important decision in your life today. God's Word may help you reach the mountaintop.

Trust in the LORD with all your heart; and lean not to your own understanding. In all your ways acknowledge Him, and He shall direct your paths. (Proverbs 3:5–6)

God will lead and teach you how to make a decision. It's even okay if we sometimes make the wrong one. It's part of the learning process. He will help us fix it, frequently using our bad decision as a detour on the road to get us to the right one. Make that decision and make it by faith.

FOCUS FOR TODAY: Let the Lord guide your steps, today and every day.

DAY 42
Prepare for Battle

READ: EPHESIANS 6:10–18

When Nehemiah and his people were building the wall in Jerusalem, they were met with much opposition from the people living in the area. Reports came to Nehemiah that attacks were planned to thwart their efforts. To protect themselves while they worked, God's people held a tool in one hand and a sword in the other. They had to be prepared for battle at any moment.

Back in that day, wars between nations and tribes were common occurrences. People always had to be prepared. It would have been silly for a warrior to go into battle with just his helmet on, leaving the rest of his body unguarded. Or to wear only his breastplate, making his head vulnerable to attack.

It's just as silly for us to go into the world without being ready. We must wear all of our spiritual armor all the time. Even when we have won a battle, the war is not over. Satan will attack again. Be prepared by putting on your armor, and you will stand against the wiles of the devil.

FOCUS FOR TODAY: Make it a habit to read or memorize and quote the armor verses from Ephesians every morning before you get out of bed.

DAY 43
Use What You've Got

READ: EXODUS 4:1–5

When the Lord called Moses to lead the children of Israel out of Egypt, Moses had nothing but a rod. Little did he know how God would use that to perform miracles before the people and bring the plagues upon Egypt that would cause Pharaoh to let God's people go.

God has always used the ordinary in someone's hands. Think of the mantle of Elijah, the widow's last bit of flour and oil, the little boy's fishes and loaves, and another widow's two mites.

In a village called Sapaterre, we started with one box of food and were soon feeding everyone there. Then, we conducted a crusade inside the village. Many were saved and God blessed us with a new church for them. A man named Charles became a Christian in Sapaterre. God gave him two cows. He named them Christ is Able and God is Good. These two cows made it possible for Charles to grow his first garden. Recently, he and his wife came to Love A Child to give an offering to the Lord, blessing us with guinea hens.

This is but a taste of what God can do when we use what He has put in our hands. God can bless whatever you have. It may be time, money, a talent, food, a prayer, or something unexpected. Our miracles may not be as impressive as those of Moses, but they will be no less important. Just use what you've got!

FOCUS FOR TODAY: What is in your hand? With God's help, use it to produce a miracle in someone's life. Then give God the glory.

DAY 44
Watch Your Words

READ: PSALM 141:1–3

I love the Haitian proverbs. They come from the old-timers who had a lot of wisdom. They say, "Little by little, the bird builds its nest" and "A little dog is really brave in front of his master's house." One proverb says, "Dirty clothes are washed in the family." That means you don't need to tell everyone everything. Don't spread your dirt around.

The Bible says, *"A talebearer reveals secrets: but he that is of a faithful spirit conceals the matter"* (Proverbs 11:13). There's nothing worse than gossiping Christians who can't keep their mouths shut. They go around spreading discord. I know some who have been hurt by that. Let's be like the faithful spirit in Proverbs and keep it between us and the Lord. Wash the dirty laundry inside the family and take the situation to the Lord in prayer.

FOCUS FOR TODAY: Pray that the Holy Spirit will guide the words you speak today and you will know when to just be quiet.

DAY 45
That Was Easy

READ: 2 KINGS 3:3–20

The king of Israel, the king of Judah, and the king of Edom were going to battle against the king of Moab. When they had gone seven days towards the battle, they realized there was no water for them or their cattle. They were facing a mighty enemy and it looked completely hopeless.

They called on Elisha, the prophet of God, who said, *"And this is but a light thing in the sight of the LORD: He will deliver the Moabites also into your hand"* (verse 18). God commanded the armies to dig ditches in the desert. The next morning, God caused water from Moab to flow into the ditches, giving them and their animals all the water they needed. Then God delivered all of Moab into their hands.

Right now, whatever problem you are feeling in your heart, whatever wilderness you are going through, know that the answer is easy for the Lord. *"Now to Him that is able to do exceeding abundantly above all that we ask or think"* (Ephesians 3:20). Trust Him.

FOCUS FOR TODAY: God is ready to intervene in any situation in your life that may seem hopeless. For God, it is easy to resolve. He can take care of your problem in a way that's greater than you can imagine.

DAY 46

Do You Have Eagle Wings or Chicken Feathers?

READ: PSALM 103:1–5

Eagles love a storm. When all of the other birds are frightened, eagles see storms as something that helps them soar. The storm's air currents lift them high above the clouds. They also depend on these currents to carry them when they get tired. Once they are soaring, they can see things more clearly.

In the same way eagles rely on the air currents, depending on God gives you the lift you need to be strong. The clarity and wisdom learned from hard times helps you weather the next storm, which may be bigger than the last. *"But they that wait upon the LORD shall renew their strength; they shall mount up with wings as eagles; they shall run, and not be weary; and they shall walk, and not faint"* (Isaiah 40:31). Use the eagle wings God gave you to rise above the storms of life. Throw away those chicken feathers!

FOCUS FOR TODAY: Sometimes, it can be hard to hold your head up during a storm. Pray that God will give you the strength to rise above it. Or pray for someone you know who is in the midst of a storm.

DAY 47
No Other Gods

READ: MATTHEW 6:19–24

Y ou shall have no other gods before Me" (Exodus 20:3). I think breaking this commandment made God angrier than anything else the children of Israel did. Just how many times did they turn their backs on God and began worshiping false gods? Too many to count.

We still have idols in our generation. They just look different. We must be careful not to have other gods before the one true God.

All Haitians love soccer. One night, we gathered all of our orphan boys together and told them, "You can love soccer, but you cannot make soccer or anything else your god. If you love soccer more than you love the Lord, it has become your god. Anything that separates us from God, brings attention to itself, and causes us to worship it, becomes a god."

Since God loves you and you are the apple of His eye, make sure you have put Him first in your life. Love Him with all your heart!

FOCUS FOR TODAY: Take an inventory of what is important to you. Look at what you spend the most time and money on. If any of those things are in danger of taking God's place in your heart, ask Him to help you change your priorities.

DAY 48
Fighting the Evil Around Us

READ: LUKE 8:26–38

For we wrestle not against flesh and blood, but against principalities, against powers, against the rulers of the darkness of this world, against spiritual wickedness in high places. (Ephesians 6:12)

Haiti is a land of voodoo, zombies, and evil spirits. One night, we had a horrible time with one of our older teenagers. She had always been sweet, normal, and church-going. In a matter of minutes, she was not the same. An evil spirit possessed her and spoke through her for many hours.

Our prayer warriors, our Haitian pastor, and others prayed. Even the rest of our children prayed and sang on the other side of the door for their sister who needed deliverance.

The evil spirit said, "I'm going to take…." Then, he proceeded to name many of our children. A number of the evil spirits named themselves and came out, but there were still more. *"This kind can come forth by nothing, but by prayer and fasting"* (Mark 9:29).

Many churches have become so modernized they don't know anything about evil spirits and the power to bind them. Living in Haiti for so long has taught us a lot about evil. The devil has some power, but Jesus has *all* power, and He has given it to us. Do not fear.

FOCUS FOR TODAY: An invisible war rages around us every day. Trusting in Jesus allows us to tap into the power God has over evil. We will win the war because Jesus overcame all.

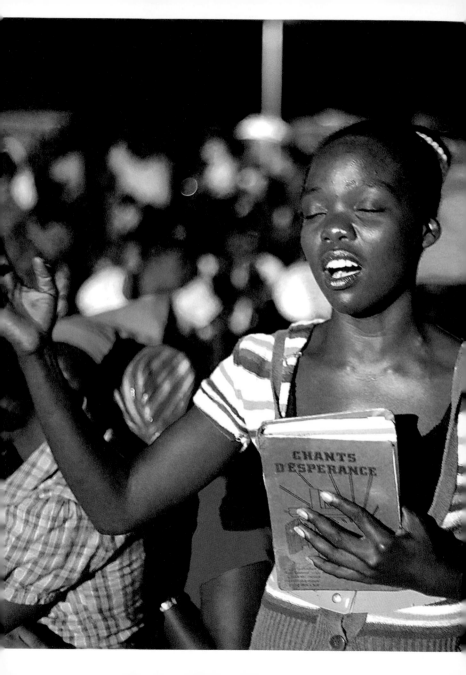

DAY 49

Four Days Late

READ: JOHN 11:1–44

In the eleventh chapter of John, we read the story of Lazarus, who was sick and near death. His sisters, Mary and Martha, sent word to Jesus, asking Him to come quickly. But after Jesus got the message, He stayed where He was for two more days. By the time Jesus arrived at his friends' house, He was four days late. Lazarus was dead and buried.

Mary and Martha were upset. Martha said, *"Lord, if You had been here, my brother had not died"* (verse 21). But Jesus spoke life into Lazarus. He came out of the grave, bound from head to foot. Jesus said, *"Loose him, and let him go"* (verse 44). What a miracle!

Sometimes, we think Jesus is late in answering our prayers. Even if He is "four days late" (or more), He's always on time for a miracle. Never doubt for a moment that God doesn't see you or answer your prayers, because He does. He truly loves and cares about you. It's going to be all right.

FOCUS FOR TODAY: When we have needs of any kind, we want God to take care of them **now**. Pray that you will trust God enough to put (and leave) your needs in His loving hands, knowing He will provide for you in His time, which is always the right time.

DAY 50
Out of the Pigpen

READ: LUKE 15:11–23

Jesus told a story about two sons. The younger one demanded his share of his father's inheritance early, went to a far country and spent it all. He found a job feeding pigs, the lowest job there was. He got so hungry that the pigs' food looked good. He decided to go home and beg his father for forgiveness.

Years ago, when we were ministering on street corners, one of our precious, godly partners, Sister Thomas, landed in the hospital. She had preached the gospel for years. When Bobby went to see her, she turned away from him and sobbed.

She said, "Brother Bobby, years ago, I drank heavy and had not done that for years. But now, I have started drinking again. I cannot go back to church or preach on the streets again."

Bobby said, "Sister Thomas, get up out of the 'pigpen,' and ask God to forgive you. Go back to work for God." That one message was what she needed to hear. Sister Thomas repented, got out of the hospital, and continued to minister until she went to be with the Lord.

We all make mistakes. We sin and mess up our lives. But we must not stay in the pigpen. God waits for us; He forgives every day and forgives completely.

FOCUS FOR TODAY: God has always been willing to forgive everyone who ever lived. No matter how mired in the pigpen you or someone you love might be, no one is outside of God's grace, mercy, and love.

DAY 51

Outnumbered

READ: 2 KINGS 6:8–18

Be strong and courageous, be not afraid nor dismayed for the king of Assyria, nor for all the multitude that is with him: for there be more with us than with him. (2 Chronicles 32:7)

On June 5, 1967, Israel was drawn into what is called the Six-Day War. They were severely outnumbered by enemies on every side. They fought Jordan, Syria, and Iraq. Their ground forces burst through Egyptian lines. On June 7, they captured the old city portion of Jerusalem and blew the ram's horn at the Western Wall. The war ended on June 10 with the Israelis victorious.

You may feel you are outnumbered today, like Israel did, and Elisha's servant in today's reading, but you cannot see the supernatural army of angels who are on your side. You may be down in a valley, but God sees you up on the mountain. You may be looking into an empty pot, but God sees your pot full and overflowing.

Do not despair. God never sees things as man sees them. He already sees the other side and it is full of blessings.

FOCUS FOR TODAY: Pray that God will open your spiritual eyes, so that you can feel the presence of His army of warriors, surrounding you and fighting for you.

DAY 52
When I See the Blood

READ: EXODUS 12:1–13

When I was a little girl growing up in a small church in Pennsylvania, we would sing a song with the refrain, "When I see the blood, I will pass, I will pass over you." I knew it had great meaning, but it wasn't until years later that I understood.

In Exodus 12, we see the last of the ten plagues the Lord brought upon the Egyptians meant to make Pharaoh let God's people go. Each firstborn child in Egypt would be killed. For their protection, God commanded the Israelites to put the blood of a sacrificed lamb on their doorposts and above the doors into their homes. When the angel of death went by, he passed over the homes that had doorways stained with blood.

Today, the blood of Jesus covers us, protects us, and, as in the words of another song, "It will never lose its power." It has power over voodoo, Satanism, and anything else the devil unleashes against us. Remember you are covered by His blood.

FOCUS FOR TODAY: Thank Jesus every day for being our sacrificial Lamb, who covers us with His blood so God passes over us on judgment day, declaring us righteous.

DAY 53
The Least of These

READ: MATTHEW 25:31–46

We recently conducted a feeding program at the large garbage dump in Cité Soleil at a place called Rapatrier. I walked into a small shanty filled with quiet, hungry children, their big eyes just staring at me. I felt the presence of Jesus and began to cry. I couldn't help it. As I held a child in my arms, I heard this over and over in my head: *"Inasmuch as you have done it to one of the least of these My brethren, you have done it to Me"* (verse 40).

On another afternoon, we visited the village of Old Letant, taking clothing and other precious items to poor children and their mothers. Many times, the children are either naked or have only a shirt to wear. The little guys we encountered were so thrilled to receive colorful undies.

Something as simple as a hot meal or a pair of underwear become great gifts. It takes so little to bless the poor. This is the very heart of God, clothing the naked and feeding the hungry. Whatever small thing you do for the poor today, you do it for Jesus.

FOCUS FOR TODAY: No matter what kind of job you have, no matter how small your income may be, God commands all of us to give something to the poor. Do what you can and the Lord will repay you.

DAY 54
The Race Is On

READ: 1 CORINTHIANS 9:24–27

Have you ever watched the Olympic running events on television, or a high school match of athletic runners? They are all in the race to win. In order to achieve their goal, they maintain a strict training regimen. The athletes learn and practice how to get rid of anything that would slow them down, especially when everyone is watching them.

We need to do the same, but our training comes in the form of prayer and studying God's Word. Our race continues on until death, or until Jesus comes and yields us an everlasting prize.

> *Wherefore seeing we also are compassed about with so great a cloud of witnesses, let us lay aside every weight, and the sin which does so easily beset us, and let us run with patience the race that is set before us.* (Hebrews 12:1)

Not only are the heavenly witnesses watching, but the eyes of the world are on us. Don't let anything slow you down or stop you as you run the race. Show the world what it looks like to be on God's team.

FOCUS FOR TODAY: Ask the Lord to give you the desire and perseverance in training to be strong in faith and life so others will want to join God's team.

DAY 55
Rich Yet Poor, or Poor and Rich?

READ: MATTHEW 19:16–23

I have been thinking a lot about riches lately. In Matthew 19, we see a rich young man come to Jesus and ask what he should do to have eternal life. Jesus tells him to keep the commandments and to love his neighbor as himself. How was the young man to do this?

If you will be perfect, go and sell that you have, and give to the poor, and you shall have treasure in heaven: and come and follow Me. But when the young man heard that saying, he went away sorrowful: for he had great possessions. (verses 21–22)

Some people condemn Christians who are rich, but I do not believe we should do this. Abraham, Isaac, Jacob, Joseph, and Job were all rich, just to name a few. It is not a sin to be rich, but it becomes a sin when riches possess us, as they did this young man. Someone once said, "God cannot give you that blessing until you first put down those things you are clutching in your hand."

God blesses those who have much and give to the poor. God blesses those who have nothing and yet give all. I believe God wants to bless us so that we can be a blessing to others. May God bless and continue to prosper you.

FOCUS FOR TODAY: Are your earthly things possessing you, or is Jesus your dearest, most precious treasure?

DAY 56
Beware of Pride

READ: EZEKIEL 26:1–21

You can spot a proud spirit in a person a mile away. *"Pride goes before destruction, and a haughty spirit before a fall"* (Proverbs 16:18).

The ancient city of Tyre was one of the wealthiest in the world in Bible times. But the heart of its king was proud and haughty, like Satan himself. In Ezekiel 26, God spoke harsh words of judgment regarding Tyre. He planned Tyre's destruction, stating He would make her *"like the top of a rock. It shall be a place for the spreading of nets in the midst of the sea"* (verses 4–5). God also declared that this city would end up under water.

Nebuchadnezzar, the king of Babylon, came first to destroy it. Two hundred fifty years later, Alexander the Great dealt the final blow. The city of Tyre to this day has never been rebuilt. It remains at the bottom of the Mediterranean Sea.

The tale of Tyre is a real wakeup call. All of us have pride hidden (or maybe not so hidden) somewhere in our hearts. In order to please God, we need to root it out. God *"resists the proud, but gives grace to the humble"* (James 4:6). I don't know about you, but I'd much rather be humble than end up at the bottom of the ocean!

FOCUS FOR TODAY: Ask God to reveal any pride in your heart so you can repent of it. Ask Him to help you follow Jesus's example of humility.

DAY 57
Be Faithful in the Small Things

READ: MATTHEW 25:14–30

We had a ministry friend with great talents. Among other gifts, he could sing and play the organ. He felt the calling to be a pastor and talked to us about what he wanted to do in the future. We said, "With your talent, you could have a wonderful church. Why don't you start small and God will build it?"

He said, "Well, if God gives me a large church of two thousand people, I will do it." He never got that church and never went far in his ministry because he refused to start with small things.

When I came to the Lord, I was sixteen years old and on fire! In my mind, I saw myself as a big preacher right away, preaching to thousands. Guess what? The Lord told me to go to my pastor and ask if I could clean the toilets of the church. I did that for months.

Mother Teresa once said, "God has not called me to be successful. He has called me to be faithful." Everyone wants to do great things and be noticed, but the Lord wants us to learn to be faithful first.

Each day, God does big and small things for us. *"For who has despised the day of small things?"* (Zechariah 4:10). God blesses small, faithful things in a big way. What will God ask you to do today?

FOCUS FOR TODAY: If we can't be faithful with the little things, how can the Lord trust us with the big things? Learn to be faithful with a few small things *and He will bless* your efforts.

DAY 58
Seven Promises

READ: PSALM 41:1–3

In these verses, the Lord has made seven promises to those who bless and help the poor. Let's take a look at them.

1. The Lord will deliver him in times of trouble.

2. The Lord will keep him safe.

3. The Lord will keep him alive.

4. He will be blessed upon the earth.

5. The Lord will not deliver him to the will of his enemies.

6. The Lord will strengthen him upon his bed of languishing.

7. The Lord will make all his bed in his sickness (restore him).

Many Christians still don't get it. Jesus allowed the poor to be placed in front of our eyes and our hearts to see what we would do. The poor man sleeping on the street under some newspapers may be Jesus. The hungry child you see on television or in your neighborhood may be Jesus.

Helping the poor and defending the fatherless and needy brings joy to your heart. It is the secret to true spiritual riches. Let the Lord use you today to bless the poor. In return, God will bless you more than you can ever imagine. Just keep your heart open.

FOCUS FOR TODAY: Look for a person in need whom you can help today, even if it's only in a small way.

DAY 59
Miracle Meals

READ: 1 KINGS 17:7–16

In the midst of a severe famine, God told Elijah to go to a widow's house in the town of Zarephath. When he arrived, the widow had only a handful of meal and a little oil.

Oh, really? How is God going to meet my need with that? That thought may have crossed Elijah's mind. Maybe he'd hoped God would send him to the home of a rich man who could take good care of him. Instead, God sent him to this poor widow who was getting ready to gather a handful of sticks, bake her last cake, share it with her son, then wait to die.

Imagine her surprise when Elijah told her to make that last cake and give it to him. When she obeyed, God refilled her meal barrel and oil jar with an unending supply. It lasted until the famine ended, just as Elijah had said.

We always think God will move in the way that makes the most sense to us. But God's ways are not our ways. He wants us to know He is still the God of miracles who can use what He wants and who He wants, whenever He wants. Never be afraid to give to the Lord, even when it's something small, or your last handful of meal. He will never fail you.

FOCUS FOR TODAY: Say, "Lord, I need a miracle. You know how to make it happen. You are the God of miracles. I don't care how You do it. I just want to thank You ahead of time for doing it Your way."

DAY 60
Our God Is Greater

READ: ISAIAH 43:1–13

Living in Haiti, we know what fear can do to someone. It can kill people or even drive them crazy. But we have the power to bind any spirit the devil throws at us. Jesus said, *"Behold, I give to you power to tread on serpents and scorpions, and over all the power of the enemy: and nothing shall by any means hurt you"* (Luke 10:19).

Years ago, when we first moved to Haiti, a sixteen-year-old girl was sold to some voodoo people. It was said that she had died and been made into a zombie. I cannot begin to tell you what she experienced. I visited her in a Haitian hospital, and when she was released from there, she had nowhere to go, so we took her into our children's home.

A Haitian pastor prayed over her every day and bound the evil powers. We saw the power of God in action. The girl was set free. How great is our God?

> *Believe Me, and understand that I am He: before Me there was no God formed, neither shall there be after Me. I, even I, am the* LORD; *and beside Me there is no savior.* (Isaiah 43:10–11)

That says it all. God existed before time began and always will be our only Lord. Beside Him, there is no other. He is the One we serve and the One who gives us the same power.

FOCUS FOR TODAY: Take some time to praise God for who He is. Thank Him for His great power and that He gives us access to it through Jesus.

DAY 61
Getting Ready for War

READ: JEREMIAH 12:1–5

I have shared this Scripture many times, but the Lord said, "Say it again!"

> *If you have run with the footmen, and they have wearied you, then how can you contend with horses? and if in the land of peace, wherein you trusted, they wearied you, then how will you do in the swelling of Jordan?* (verse 5)

Let's face it. God is not raising an army of sissies. He's training us for war. He does this by letting certain things knock us down to see if we will get back up. If we struggle to deal with the little battles and they weary us, what will we do when the big ones come? The battles over good (God's way) and evil (Satan's way) will continue until the day we die.

He allows this to happen because He loves us. He wants us to learn to get back on our feet and finish the fight. If we cannot overcome the lion and the bear, we'll never kill the giant. Remember what happens in the end: We win! Do not be afraid. Stand your ground. Help is on the way.

FOCUS FOR TODAY: Pray for strength and guidance in your daily battles, both small and big. As God gives us victories, He teaches us strategies to use in the next battle.

DAY 62
Give Me Patience—Now!

READ: PSALM 27:7–14

Have you ever been impatient with the Lord? God made a promise to Abraham when he was old that he would have a son with his wife, Sarah, who was barren. As they both grew older together, Sarah got tired of waiting on the Lord. She told Abraham to have a child with her Egyptian maid, Hagar. So Ishmael was born, but he was not the son that God promised. Abraham was one hundred years old when Isaac, the seed of the promise, was finally born.

Like Sarah, have you ever tried to do something your way, instead of God's way? We always mess it up. If we wait on the Lord, He has a better way and He is always on time.

For as the heavens are higher than the earth, so are My ways higher than your ways, and My thoughts than your thoughts.
(Isaiah 55:9)

We may not understand all of His ways, but God has a master plan for every situation in your life. It is always best to completely turn it over to the Lord. Let God do it right.

FOCUS FOR TODAY: We live in an impatient, instantaneous world. Ask the Lord to slow you down and teach you to wait for the revelation of His perfect plans in His perfect time.

DAY 63
It Is Well

READ: 2 KINGS 4:8–37

One of my favorite hymns is one written in the late 1800s by Horatio Spafford. A lawyer and wealthy businessman, he loved and trusted the Lord. God blessed him with many investments, a loving wife, four daughters, and a young son.

But Horatio was like Job. His son died from pneumonia at age two. In 1871, Horatio lost everything he had in the Great Chicago Fire. Two years later, after regaining some of his finances, he planned a trip to Europe with his wife and daughters. At the last minute, he could not go. During that trip, the ship carrying his family collided with another ship, and his four young daughters drowned. Horatio received a cable from his wife that read, "Saved alone." Later, he wrote the wonderful song, "It Is Well with My Soul." The first verse speaks to all of us:

> When peace, like a river, attendeth my way,
> When sorrows like sea billows roll:
> Whatever my lot, Thou hast taught me to know,
> It is well, it is well with my soul.

One day, I heard one of our Haitian workers singing this song in French. It brought tears to my eyes because I hope I can sing that when my trial comes. Today, you may be going through a trial and can't see the other side. The Lord is saying to you, "It is well."

FOCUS FOR TODAY: Read the lyrics to this great hymn online or watch one of the many YouTube videos of it.

DAY 64

So You Think You Want to Be a Missionary?

READ: MATTHEW 9:35–38

Bobby and I have seen many missionaries, or people who thought they were missionaries, come and go in Haiti.

There is a big difference between having a desire and having a true calling to be a missionary. If we only have the desire, then when it gets hot, everything goes wrong, and voodoo powers are all around us, one may weaken. When money is tight, and death, starvation, and emergencies happen all around you, the desire quickly leaves.

One who has the true calling of God to be a missionary will not be stopped.

> *How beautiful upon the mountains are the feet of him that brings good tidings…, that publishes salvation.* (Isaiah 52:7)

There are fewer and fewer missionaries in the field each day. Many are called to do things for the Lord and some are called to be missionaries. Do you have the calling? Maybe God is calling you to hike up mountains, cross rivers, walk through a garbage dump, or crawl on your hands and knees inside a cave to get to the poor.

FOCUS FOR TODAY: Whether or not you are called to the mission field, you should consider giving time to a third world country. Whether you go to preach the gospel, feed the hungry, help with a building project, or work in a mobile medical clinic, your life will never be the same. It will be better.

DAY 65
Obedience Is Better than Sacrifice

READ: PSALM 40:4–8

In Genesis 6:14, God spoke to Noah and said, "Build an ark." Noah did not question or argue with God, but for many years, he pounded away, building the ark, while others made fun of him.

Abraham obeyed in faith when he was called to go to a place he didn't know. Joshua obeyed when God commanded him to go in and possess the Promised Land.

These and many other heroes of the faith obeyed God above all else. God loves your obedience more than your offerings. *"Has the LORD as great delight in burnt offerings and sacrifices, as in obeying the voice of the LORD? Behold, to obey is better than sacrifice, and to hearken than the fat of rams"* (1 Samuel 15:22).

Has God been speaking to your heart to do something? Have you made excuses? If we back off from the call of God, the plan of God will still go forward, but we will be set aside. Someone else will be called forward to do the job God wanted us to do. It's not a question of losing one's salvation, but of losing one's call. Our obedience is important to the Lord. Don't be afraid to do what the Lord has told you to do.

FOCUS FOR TODAY: Pray that you will trust God and have the courage to obey the Lord, regardless of what He wants you to do.

DAY 66
Burn that Bridge

READ: EXODUS 14:19–31

There was only one way to get away from Pharaoh and his army. The Egyptians chased the people of God, who ended up with the Red Sea in front of them and Pharaoh's chariots at their heels. Moses prayed and stretched out his hands. The waters parted until all of God's people made it across. As soon as Pharaoh's army got right in the middle of the seabed, God allowed the Red Sea to come back and swallow up every soldier in the Egyptian army.

Despite this great miracle, God knew it wouldn't be long before the Israelites wished they were back in Egypt. God burned the bridge behind them so there was no way for them to go back.

Sometimes, that's what our loving God does. He burns bridges behind us so we won't be able to return to the past. We may need to leave certain relationships, homes, employers, or other situations. Be assured it's because He has better things ahead.

FOCUS FOR TODAY: When God opens the Red Sea and you walk to the other side, don't look back. Embrace every new and better thing God has planned for you.

DAY 67
But I'm Hungry

READ: JAMES 2:14–18

When Bobby and I started working in Haiti, we thought we were going to win everyone we met for the Lord. We offered pastor's seminars, held crusades, and preached to Haitians about the love of God. At one crusade, a mother held her malnourished baby high in the air and yelled in Creole, "If God is so good, why is my baby so hungry?"

That was our turning point. From then on, Love A Child began feeding hungry and starving children. Galatians 6:9 teaches us not to be weary *"in well doing: for in due season we shall reap, if we faint not."* Feeding hungry families can be difficult. Sometimes people become frightened that there will not be enough food for them. Fights can easily break out. But we cannot be discouraged.

We share what God blesses us with each month. Thanks to our Love A Child partners and Feed My Starving Children, we feed thousands of schoolchildren each day, provide monthly food supplies for those in our feeding programs, and distribute food to over ninety organizations and missionaries throughout Haiti. About half are orphan homes that really depend upon this monthly food.

We must feed them first, then they will open their hearts. Love is something you do.

FOCUS FOR TODAY: Consider doing what you can to feed the hungry. It may be donating money to a relief organization, dropping off food at your local food bank, or helping to serve meals at a homeless shelter.

DAY 68

Pick Up Your Cross and Follow Me

READ: LUKE 9:23–27

We all carry different crosses. There is a story about a great pile of crosses. One man thought his cross was too heavy, so he placed it on the ground and began digging through the huge pile. After searching for hours, he spotted the smallest cross and picked it up. Then he realized it was the same cross he'd brought. It turned out to be the lightest.

We live in a time now where it's all about me. I cannot deny myself anything. Instead we ask, "What can God do for me? Bless me, God." Pastor and speaker John MacArthur once said, "The true gospel is a call to self-denial. It is not a call to self-fulfillment."

Jesus said, "*If any man will come after Me, let him deny himself, and take up his cross, and follow Me*" (Matthew 16:24). This is a daily, total commitment. Are you willing to say, "I will deny myself, take up His cross, and follow Jesus all the way"? If so, then God can use you.

FOCUS FOR TODAY: Ask the Lord to help you take the focus off yourself and put it on Jesus. Pray that Jesus will show you how to follow Him better every day.

DAY 69
Clay and Potter

READ: JEREMIAH 18:1–6

I have watched Haitian people make clay pots. Their hands are so skillful. It reminds me of God.

"O Lord, you are our father; we are the clay, and You our potter; and we all are the work of Your hand" (Isaiah 64:8). We must be like clay, willing to sit there and let the hands of the Potter, Jesus, shape us. He wraps His hands around our lives, our problems, our insecurities, our hang-ups, our hurts, and our failures, molding us into that new vessel.

Sometimes the Master Potter uses trials to break our hearts so He can remake our lives into new vessels, ones that make God happy. There is a process going on that we do not understand, but we are safe in our Potter's hands.

FOCUS FOR TODAY: Use this prayer from Bobby: "Oh Lord, mold us and shape us in Thy hands. Make us what You would have us be."

DAY 70
The Solid Foundation

READ: MATTHEW 7:24–27

Bobby and I were in Haiti when the 2010 earthquake hit. It was a day I will never forget. I was in the mud-hut village of Letant; Bobby was here with all our children and staff in our two-story children's home. When the quake hit, it moved this big building back and forth with a roar. The whole children's home then went into a wave and shook like a fierce dog, shaking its head. The children and staff on the bottom floor ran out, but Bobby and Nini, one of our staff members, were stuck on the top floor. The movement knocked Bobby flat on his back, but there was not one crack in the building.

Our children's home stood strong because it was designed by a wise engineer. He said, "I am going to put in a very deep foundation. It will cost you a lot more money, but one day, when you have an earthquake, you will call me and thank me." And, we did!

Our foundation must be built on the rock of Jesus. Things in your life may be shaking you up, but you are grounded in Jesus. You will withstand the winds, storms, earthquakes, and the times of testing. When it is all over, you will be stronger and better than ever!

FOCUS FOR TODAY: Either use a hymnal or the Internet to look up some songs of faith such as "The Church's One Foundation," "How Firm a Foundation," or "The Wise Man Built His House upon a Rock."

DAY 71
Repentance

READ: ACTS 2:27–41

I went into the room the little boys share in the children's home. In the corner, about seven boys sat in a circle, praying, their hands folded and their eyes closed. The presence of the Holy Spirit filled the room.

I stood, watching for a while, amazed. I had never seen anything like this before. That evening at our children's church service, I asked Moses (age six) what they were praying about. He said, "Oh, we had a lot of sins and were asking Jesus to forgive us."

"The goodness of God leads you to repentance" (Romans 2:4). These children experienced the goodness of God when they were rescued from life-threatening situations and placed in our children's home.

People often ask us why we feed the hungry, clothe the naked, care for the sick, and provide education and housing, in addition to church growth and crusades. The answer is simple: the goodness of God leads men to repentance. We are fishing for souls.

FOCUS FOR TODAY: Examine your spirit, asking Jesus to reveal any sins for which you need forgiveness. Pray and repent.

DAY 72
You Are Always on His Mind

READ: PSALM 139:1–18

Do you realize how much time we spend thinking no one understands what we are going through or that the Lord has forgotten about us? But that's impossible! He knew you before you were born. He knows how many hairs are on your head today, and how many you had when you were younger!

We are always on His mind, every second, every minute, day and night, day after day, year after year. You cannot run from His love.

> *Where shall I go from Your Spirit? or where shall I flee from Your presence? If I ascend up into heaven, You are there: if I make my bed in hell, behold, You are there. If I take the wings of the morning, and dwell in the uttermost parts of the sea; even there shall Your hand lead me, and Your right hand shall hold me.* (verses 7–10)

He knows the battle you are facing today, your heartache, and your big decision. We serve a God who never gets tired of reaching out to us. He is never too busy to listen to our heart's cry. He has never left you. You are always on His mind and in His heart.

FOCUS FOR TODAY: Ask the Lord to help you to feel His presence. Rest in the certainty that He is right beside you all the time.

DAY 73
Stones for Remembrance

READ: JOSHUA 4:1–9

In today's reading, the Lord told Joshua to have one man from each of the twelve tribes choose a stone from the middle of the Jordan River. In order to get to the Promised Land, the Israelites had to cross the Jordan. The river was at flood stage, overflowing and impossible to cross.

Just as God opened the Red Sea so the people could escape the Egyptians and walk on dry land, He repeated that miracle at the Jordan River. God wanted His people to pick up stones and stack them on the other side. They were to look at these stones, remember, and say, "Look what the Lord did for me!"

Bobby and I still have a grocery receipt from the Caribbean Market that is dated January 12, 2010. We had gone to buy food for our team and left just a short time before the earthquake hit. It crushed everything and everyone inside that market.

Do you have "stones" to remember what God has done for you? Thank Him now.

FOCUS FOR TODAY: If you don't already do this, start collecting memory "stones." You can save meaningful objects (like our receipt), write God's blessings on slips of paper to keep in a jar or folder, jot down events in a journal—whatever works to help you keep track of the good things that God has done for you.

DAY 74
Fiery Coals

READ: LUKE 6:27–36

The first time we hired Mezelus, he was so mean. We had a big fight and we had to fire him. Soon after that, he became very ill, so we put him in the best hospital in Haiti and took care of him.

Once he was better, he visited our church. When the message ended, he came forward for salvation and wanted to say something. He spoke of our kindness to him. Because of that, he wanted to be converted. We rehired Mezelus and he still works for us at our children's home. I often think of how God turned our enemy into this sweet, precious man.

> *If your enemy be hungry, give him bread to eat; and if he be thirsty, give him water to drink: for you shall heap coals of fire upon his head, and the* Lord *shall reward you.*
>
> (Proverbs 25:21–22)

We don't give, feed the poor, or bless our enemies to get something back. We do it because that is what Jesus would do. Don't worry about your enemies. Just bless them in the name of the Lord and go on. God's blessings come automatically.

FOCUS FOR TODAY: Starting today, pray daily for an enemy, or someone who is giving you trouble.

DAY 75
Not in that Dirty River

READ: 2 KINGS 5:1–14

Naaman was a mighty man of valor, a captain in the army of the king of Syria. But he was also a leper. One of the servant girls who took care of Naaman's wife told her about a prophet of God who could heal leprosy. Naaman went to see Elisha, who sent a messenger to tell Naaman to dip seven times in the river Jordan and he would be healed.

Naaman did not want to bathe in the dirty Jordan. Full of pride and anger, Naaman first demanded to know why Elisha had sent a messenger instead coming to see him personally. In addition, Naaman did not want to step into the dirty Jordan. He wanted to wash in a cleaner river and turned to leave. One of Naaman's servants convinced him to try it. So Naaman came back and did it. When he came out of the Jordan for the seventh time, he was healed.

Sometimes, the Lord tells us to do something that may not make sense or is downright unpleasant. He is looking for complete obedience. We may not want to bathe in the dirty river either, preferring to wash in a cleaner one. Do it anyway. Your blessing comes in obedience.

FOCUS FOR TODAY: Trust that God has a reason for wanting you to take on a challenge or task that may be unpleasant or not make any sense to you. Rest in the assurance that it will be for your benefit in the long run.

DAY 76
Good Measure

READ: DEUTERONOMY 15:7–11

God measures your giving. I love this Scripture: *"Give, and it shall be given to you; good measure, pressed down, and shaken together, and running over"* (Luke 6:38).

When we buy something on the streets in Haiti, we watch the machann (market women) pour flour, rice, beans, or other goods into "mamit" measuring cans. The ladies always make sure it is piled high on top and running over the sides.

When we give to Jesus, He never cheats us. He gives us back a good measure for our generosity. He presses it down, shakes it, puts more in, then lets it run over the sides. And just think, there are some people afraid to give.

Many of God's people are not stingy. If we honor the Lord with what we have and bless others with it, the Lord will bless us. Bobby always says, "Jesus gives back more on our money than the banks do." Delight in the joy of giving.

FOCUS FOR TODAY: Determine how much you can give to your church or a Christian organization. Then add a little more so it overflows!

DAY 77
Just a Touch

READ: MARK 5:25–34

A multitude surrounded Jesus as he walked to Jairus's house to save his little daughter. Among them was a woman who had been bleeding for twelve years. When Jesus came through the area, the crowd thronged all around, but she was desperate and determined. She knew by faith that He wouldn't even have to pray for her. If she could just get close enough to touch the hem of His garment, she believed she would be healed. She did—and she was.

Jesus felt her faith as it touched the virtue in Him. He turned and asked, "Who touched My clothes?" The disciples pointed out that hundreds were touching Him. How did Jesus expect them to narrow it down to one single person? What Jesus meant was, who had touched Him in faith?

At this moment, so many prayers are being said all over the world. Will your prayer touch Jesus? *"Now faith is the substance of things hoped for, the evidence of things not seen"* (Hebrews 11:1). Yes, it will, if you reach out in faith. Hope without faith is just an empty wish. But when you add real, Bible-believing faith to hope, you have the evidence that it already exists.

No matter how bad things look, remember, all it takes is one touch from the Master. Let's walk in faith today

FOCUS FOR TODAY: Pray that you will have faith the size of a mustard seed, then ask, like the disciples did, for Jesus to increase it.

DAY 78
Ashamed of the Gospel?

READ: 2 TIMOTHY 1:8–12

People in today's world are not ashamed of anything they do. Many things are too vulgar to repeat. People brag about doing drugs, having affairs, and worse.

The apostle Paul suffered many things. He had been beaten, tortured, imprisoned, and shipwrecked. His days were coming to an end, knowing he would soon be beheaded for the gospel's sake. He said, *"For I am not ashamed of the gospel of Christ: for it is the power of God to salvation"* (Romans 1:16).

In the end, God is the great equalizer. He brings down the proud and lifts up the beggar. He makes us all the same. One day, everyone will face Jesus, and *"every knee should bow...and every tongue should confess that Jesus Christ is Lord"* (Philippians 2:10–11).

Before He left this earth, Jesus commanded us to preach the gospel to every living creature. Paul knew everyone needed to hear about Jesus. The Lord wants to use you and me. We must be bold, not ashamed, of spreading the gospel. No one should have to appear in front of Jesus without having heard of Him.

FOCUS FOR TODAY: Turn to God for guidance and courage to share the gospel today. Then let the Holy Spirit lead you to someone who needs to hear the good news.

DAY 79
Burdens

READ: MATTHEW 11:28–30

Often, when we are hiking up the steep mountains under the heat of the tropical sun, carrying backpacks or whatever else we need, a precious Haitian comes along. He takes our load and helps us make it up the mountain.

At other times, we recognize the many burdens facing the Haitians. The devastating situations of these poor people can be overwhelming.

In order for us to be effective for God, we must always be mindful to cast those burdens on the Lord and let Him sustain us. If we feel tired and worn down, it could mean we are trying to do things on our own.

"Cast your burden upon the LORD, and He shall sustain you: He shall never allow the righteous to be moved" (Psalm 55:22). It feels so good to have someone help us carry our load up the mountain. Jesus wants to do that for you today. Stay close to the Lord. It makes life so much easier.

FOCUS FOR TODAY: We tend to think we can do it all and handle it all. Ask the Lord to help you place the burdens in your life on Him and let Him take care of things.

DAY 80
Remember to Pray

READ: MATTHEW 6:8–33

Thanks to our ministry partners, we had been able to build a new orphanage for Madamn Adeline, a dear Haitian woman who has taken in many orphans over the years. They were having church under an old sheet and piece of plastic. Another of our faithful partners donated money to build a church next to the new orphanage. Later, we learned that one little orphan living there would start praying at 4:00 a.m. each morning, asking the Lord to give them a new church!

This sweet child trusted completely that God would answer his prayer. And God already knew of their need for a church. When we put God first, we don't need to worry if He hears us because He already knows what we need before we ask Him.

We live in the day of social media, emails, text messages, iPads, and more. It is so important for us not to let these modern inventions of man take us away from our time of prayer and being in God's presence. Sometimes, that's exactly what happens—and we suffer for it. *"You have not, because you ask not"* (James 4:2).

Keep your focus on God. Spend intentional time with Him. Pray without ceasing. Then your day will be truly blessed!

FOCUS FOR TODAY: Our lives are so noisy and busy that it is easy to neglect a time of prayer. Decide to make a change today. Choose a time, a quiet place, and keep a daily appointment with God.

DAY 81
Don't Look Back

READ: PHILIPPIANS 3:12–16

Once I visited a Christian brother in the hospital who had a big family problem with his wife. He had gotten drunk and crashed into a tree. He felt like his life was washed up. I told him that the Lord forgives sin. He needed to repent, move forward, and serve the Lord.

Some people keep their focus on things in the past: a failed marriage, a lost job, someone who did them wrong, and the list goes on. It's kind of like driving while only looking in the car's rearview mirror rather than through the windshield.

When Jesus comes into our lives, we must let Him keep us focused on the good things ahead. Paul wrote, *"Forgetting those things which are behind, and reaching forth to those things which are before, I press toward the mark"* (verses 13–14).

Stop looking at where you have been and start looking at where you are going. Everything you have ever wanted is ahead of you, not behind you. The Lord has better things ahead. Press toward the mark. The best is yet to come.

FOCUS FOR TODAY: We all have a hard time letting go of certain things in our past. Ask the Lord to help you put those things behind you, once and for all. Keep your focus on Jesus and what He has planned for your future.

DAY 82
People Are Not Our Enemies

READ: EPHESIANS 6:10–12

For many years, Bobby and I had attacks from a certain person who was extremely jealous of our work here in Haiti and hated us without cause. We have also had some major weapons thrown at us through the years. These included death threats and any number of voodoo curses. One of them involved a small, wooden coffin that was placed on the road in front of our Love A Child Children's Home.

At first, we didn't realize who our real enemy was. It was not any man, but the spirit behind the man.

For we wrestle not against flesh and blood, but against princi-palities, against powers, against the rulers of the darkness of this world, against spiritual wickedness in high places. (verse 12)

Satan will assign spirits from hell to distract, delay, discourage and derail your efforts to do what God has called you to do. It is important to be strong, stand unafraid, and refuse to be intimidated by the enemy. Because Jesus is with us, they cannot hurt us, their weapons won't work, and that jealous or evil person will not prosper.

FOCUS FOR TODAY: When the devil starts messing, God starts blessing! Thank the Lord today for His mercy, love, and protection.

DAY 83
Our Unchanging God

READ: HEBREWS 1:8–12

Have you ever run into someone you haven't seen in years? The first thing you may think is, *Wow, they've sure changed.* Maybe they look or act different. Change surrounds us. The church is changing, the world is changing, the thoughts and attitudes of people are changing, and Haiti is changing.

But our God never changes. Today's reading in Hebrews is amazing! And how about Psalm 102:25–27?

> *Of old have You laid the foundation of the earth: and the heavens are the work of Your hands. They shall perish, but You shall endure: yea, all of them shall wax old like a garment; as a vesture shall You change them, and they shall be changed: but You are the same, and Your years shall have no end.*

We may talk a lot and not mean what we say, or promise to do things and not follow through. But God always means what He says, says what He means, and does what He promises. We serve the one and only invincible God, who always has been, always will be, never changing, a miracle-working God. There is one thing we can know for certain: He is always the same wonderful God!

FOCUS FOR TODAY: *"Jesus Christ the same yesterday, and to day, and for ever"* (Hebrews 13:8). If you have a change in your life that's bothering you, rest in the comfort of knowing that God never changes and He's always there for you.

DAY 84
Life Is Short

READ: ECCLESIASTES 3:1–8

One morning, I woke up at 3:00 a.m. and listened to our clock ticking away. Time doesn't stop for anyone. It just keeps moving on. Every minute that goes by means we are closer to the coming of the Lord or our death.

God knows the length of our days. Your calling, your ministry, or your assignment from the Lord takes time. Life is so short that we must make every day count for Him and not waste it. In his poem, "Only One Life," C. T. Studd wrote, "Only what's done for Christ will last."

None of us knows how much time we have. Only God knows that. We may die or Jesus may return today. *"For what is your life? It is even a vapor, that appears for a little time, and then vanishes away"* (James 4:14).

No matter which way He comes for us, let's make sure He finds us working and being faithful to Him. Are you ready?

FOCUS FOR TODAY: Our time is in His hands. Share some of your time today with someone who needs you.

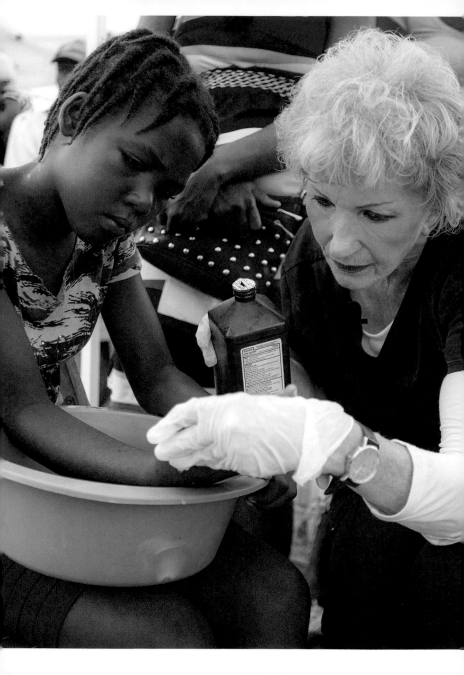

DAY 85
God Has a Better Plan

READ: ROMANS 11:33–36

For months, we had planned a mobile medical clinic in the mountains of Peyi Pouri. It is a hard place to get to, and it takes tough four-wheel-drive vehicles that can climb a coconut tree! Thousands come and depend on our mobile medical clinics. Even though we'd planned this one for October—well past the rainy season of May through July—the rains came. It took out the entire road to Peyi Pouri. We had to change locations quickly.

We decided to go to Lastik—through the mountain, down into the riverbed, and up the mountain again—but discovered the roads were washed out there, too. We headed to La Roche, but those roads were also washed out. We finally ended up at Chambrun, a voodoo village.

Our next clinic was to be in Cotin, but all we found were impassible, muddy roads. So, we decided to try again, believing the roads would be dry enough to go on.

Why does God change our plans? We don't know. We only know that His ways are higher and better than our ways. *"Neither are your ways My ways"* (Isaiah 55:8).

We walk by faith and not by sight.

FOCUS FOR TODAY: Be ready for a change in plans at any moment!

DAY 86
Under His Wings

READ: PSALM 91

A while back, there was a dangerous man and his family living in an area we oversee known as Le Tant (Kingdom Connection) Village. He had been causing a great deal of trouble and threatened many of the village people with death. He threatened us, too. There was no doubt that he would come after us. We made the decision to have the judge and police remove this man and his family, and filled out the appropriate paperwork. We were at peace, despite his threats. The Lord is our protector and watches over us.

In the days and times in which we live, there is violence and evil all over the earth. His Word promises that He is always with us and will protect us. Being in the presence of the Lord is the safest place to be, especially in times of trouble.

"He shall cover you with His feathers, and under His wings shall you trust: His truth shall be your shield and buckler" (verse 4). When we hide ourselves where the Lord dwells, He will protect us from evil just as a hen cares for her chicks.

FOCUS FOR TODAY: Whenever you find yourself in danger, call on the Lord for protection, then run to the safety of His loving arms.

DAY 87
Share and Share Alike

READ: 1 SAMUEL 30:21–25

David and six hundred men in his army had been pursuing the Amalekites for a number of days. After they had stopped and rested, two hundred of them were too exhausted to continue. But when David and the four hundred defeated their enemy, David commanded that the plunder be divided among all of the men, not just the ones who had physically been in the battle.

God knows that not everyone can go into the mission field, or is called to do so. If the Lord does call you, He also calls people to sustain you. These partners support you by their prayers, donations, and help in many ways. *"But as his part is that goes down to the battle, so shall his part be that tarries by the stuff: they shall part alike"* (verse 24).

This means that when Bobby and I go to the mountains and regions beyond to win a witch doctor over to the Lord, or feed a hungry child, or care for the sick and dying, our ministry partners share in every soul that is won for Jesus, every child who is fed, and every life that is saved. The results belong to all of us. Regardless of who goes or who stays, we are in this together!

FOCUS FOR TODAY: Spend some extra time in prayer for any missionary you know. Is God calling you to do something more?

DAY 88
The Body of Christ

READ: 1 CORINTHIANS 12:14–27

We know this Scripture talks about the foot, the ear, and the eye, but my attention goes to the *"uncomely parts"* (verse 23) of the body that no one sees. Without them, we wouldn't be alive.

I'm pretty sure no one ever stopped you to remark, "My, you have a wonderful pancreas" or "Wow, what a great esophagus." The parts of the body we don't see are frequently the most important. Unless you're going barefoot or wearing sandals, most people won't get to see your big toe, which is really fairly small when you think about it. But it's that toe that helps to give you balance.

> *If the whole body were an eye, where were the hearing? If the whole were hearing, where were the smelling? But now has God set the members every one of them in the body, as it has pleased Him.* (verses 17–18)

You may feel like you are so small, so insignificant, or your offering is so small that it can't possibly do anyone any good. Not true! You are so, so important to the rest of the body of Christ. God has put you right where He wants you!

FOCUS FOR TODAY: Thank the Lord for where He has put you. Ask Him for wisdom and encouragement to be more effective in the work He has for you.

DAY 89
A Light on a Hill

READ: MATTHEW 5:14–16

I woke up early this morning thinking about lighthouses. I've always loved them. D. L. Moody said, "Lighthouses don't fire cannons to call attention to their shining—they just shine."

We recently finished building a new church on top of a high mountain in Peyi Pouri. That means "rotten country," but now the people call it Peyi Beni, which means "the blessed country." A huge, solar-lit cross stands on the edge of the mountain cliff, visible for miles. It acts like a lighthouse on the mountain! *"You are the light of the world. A city that is set on a hill cannot be hidden"* (verse 14).

The world is watching you and me. Showing God's kindness and love in our actions may be the only Bible some people read. We are the lights here in Haiti. You are the lights in your corner of the earth. Let Jesus's light shine through you today.

FOCUS FOR TODAY: Most of us know the proverb, "Actions speak louder than words." Make sure your actions today are consistent with God's love and reflect the life-giving light of Christ.

DAY 90
In the Valley

READ: PSALM 23

It is easy to praise God when things in our lives are going well. When we go through the valley, though, we seem to lose faith.

We have a pastor friend named Ron. His favorite song is "God on the Mountain" by Bill and Gloria Gaither. Ron's wife and his teenaged son were killed in car accidents.

At his son's funeral, Ron bravely got up and sang, "For the God on the mountain, is the God in the valley. When things go wrong, He'll make them right." I still cry when I think of Ron singing that song. Today, he is remarried and has another son.

Be not afraid, neither be you dismayed: for the LORD your God is with you wherever you go.   (Joshua 1:9)

The Lord is always on your side. When you go through that valley, if you're going through a divorce, sickness, family problems, death, financial problems, or anything else, don't be afraid or discouraged. The Lord is with you. Our God is the God of the good times and the God of the bad times. He is always God!

FOCUS FOR TODAY: While we know and believe the Lord is by our side through everything, we also need the physical and emotional support of Christian friends when we're in a valley. Pray for someone you know in a difficult situation. Put your love in action by sending a note, getting groceries, or anything you can do to ease their suffering.

About the Authors

Bobby and Sherry Burnette are the founders and directors of Love A Child, Inc. (LAC), a 501(c)(3) Christian nonprofit humanitarian organization serving the needs of children in Haiti. They began their ministry together in the late 1960s by preaching on street corners, under gospel tents, and in auditoriums and churches throughout the United States. In 1971, Bobby and Sherry made their first missions trip to Haiti, and the overwhelming poverty they witnessed there broke their hearts. They also ministered in many other countries, but they always found themselves drawn back to Haiti. Following their calling from God, Bobby and Sherry founded Love A Child in 1985 and focused on working to reduce poverty in Haiti's remote areas.

From their beginnings as visiting missionaries to Haiti, Bobby and Sherry have worked to spread the Word of God and show the love of Jesus by example through feeding programs, mobile medical clinics, and the building of Christian schools and churches. They moved to Haiti in 1991 and have never looked back, living year-round at the Love A Child Children's Home in Fond Parisien, Haiti.

Love A Child's outreach programs include: a 21,500-square-foot children's home, now home to eighty-five children; primary schools that educate and feed more than eight thousand five hundred children each day; mobile medical clinics; a regional medical clinic; and a feeding distribution program that serves more than 25 million meals every year. After the devastating 2010 earthquake in Haiti, Love A Child built over five hundred houses for earthquake victims and developed eight sustainability projects, including *Gwo Maché Mirak*, a large marketplace providing jobs for the poor; *Poul Mirak*, a project to train Haitians how to raise and sell chickens; a tilapia fish farm; and an agricultural training center that teaches the farming of crops and trees. Bobby and Sherry believe that feeding the poor is essential, but that the ultimate goal is for Haitians to become self-sustaining.

Under the Burnettes' leadership, Love A Child has grown to become one of the largest Christian nonprofits in Haiti. Thanks to LAC's excellence in financial accountability, the organization consistently receives the highest industry ratings available through the Evangelical Council for Financial Accountability (ECFA), Charity Navigator, and the Independent Charities of America. In 2015, they documented the story of their ministry in their first book, *Love Is Something You Do*, with Whitaker House.

Bobby and Sherry want people to know what faith and love can do to change a nation. It is their deepest desire that their lives inspire others to reach out in response to the cry of the poor in some way, large or small—rescuing one child at a time.